PRAISE FOR GRIP

"GRIP helps me get more done and then really unplug when I'm not working. Super inspiring!"
—ANNA DRIJVER, ACTRESS FROM
THE NETFLIX ORIGINAL *UNDERCOVER*

• • •

"GRIP packs a punch with powerful strategies that will reinvent your ability to get more done than ever."
—JEFF SANDERS, KEYNOTE SPEAKER AND
AUTHOR OF *THE 5 AM MIRACLE*

• • •

"GRIP helped me get annoying tasks under control, like keeping up with emails and invoices, and then helped me map out and pursue the goals that make my life more meaningful."
—LOIS VAN BAARLE (LOISH), DIGITAL ARTIST
AND CHARACTER DESIGNER

• • •

"A practical approach for getting more done."
—ALI NIKNAM, CEO OF BUNQ

• • •

"This is one of those books you don't just read and put aside. It keeps on giving: a clear guide to turn to daily. Implement Rick's practical suggestions and start making smarter decisions—both professionally and in other parts of your life."
—MARK DE LANGE, FOUNDER AND CEO OF ACE & TATE

• • •

"Finally! A sane and down-to-earth manual to help you get the most out of your workweek. I don't know of a book that gives you this many spot-on tips."
—ERNST-JAN PFAUTH, COFOUNDER AND CEO
OF THE CORRESPONDENT

• • •

"Rick has completely reimagined the strategy for your calendar, email, and to-do list. His tips are clear and accessible, and his approach is genius. This is a book I wish I'd had ten years ago."

—BORIS VELDHUIJZEN VAN ZANTEN, FOUNDER AND CEO OF THE NEXT WEB

• • •

"GRIP is a book to turn to often: I love the structure it brings to my workweek. Rick's strategic approach is remarkably relevant for anyone."

—TACO CARLIER, COFOUNDER AND CEO OF VANMOOF

RICK PASTOOR

GRIP

The art of working smart
(and getting to what matters most)

**Translated from the Dutch by
Elizabeth Manton and Erica Moore**

HarperCollins
Leadership

An Imprint of HarperCollins

First published in Dutch as *Grip: het geheim van slim werken* by
Uitgeverij NZ in 2019

Copyright © 2019 by Rick Pastoor

English translation copyright © 2021 Erica Moore and Elizabeth Manton

Published by HarperCollins Leadership, an imprint of HarperCollins Focus LLC.

Any internet addresses, phone numbers, or company or product information
printed in this book are offered as a resource and are not intended in any way
to be or to imply an endorsement by HarperCollins Leadership, nor does
HarperCollins Leadership vouch for the existence, content, or services of these
sites, phone numbers, companies, or products beyond the life of this book.

Translation copyright © 2022 Erica Moore and Elizabeth Manton
Ilustrations by Moker Ontwerp and Rick Pastoor

ISBN 978-1-4002-3369-4 (eBook)
ISBN 978-1-4002-3368-7 (TP)

Library of Congress Control Number: 2021952500

Printed in the United States of America
22 23 24 25 26 LSC 10 9 8 7 6 5 4 3 2 1

CONTENTS

PART 3
GRIP AND YOUR LIFE

INTRODUCTION

When you consider what a huge role work plays in our lives, it's strange we're never really taught how to do it. Working is just supposed to come naturally. As if we all magically know how to set priorities, juggle a schedule, make good plans, and stay on top of a busy job. These skills may sound simple, but they're not.

Perhaps, like me, you're familiar with the signs that work's not going your way. The week has barely started and already you're playing catch-up. At the end of another long workday your inbox is still overflowing. On top of that, your calendar is jam-packed and your to-do list goes on forever. It's enough to break anybody's spirit. The worst part is that when you start to feel like you're losing your grip on your days, it can be paralyzing. And just try getting any work done after that. No wonder you have trouble meeting the targets you set, struggle to deliver the quality you aspire to, and can't ever seem to get around to personal development. You're working hard, but are you making any progress?

Believe me, I've been there. For nearly six years I was the head of product at Blendle, a Dutch company that was lauded internationally for coming up with new business models for journalism. I joined the startup as a programmer at age twenty-five, after selling the software agency I founded and ran for six years. At Blendle things moved pretty fast. We managed to get big titles like the *Economist* and the *Wall Street Journal* on board. We got backing from Axel Springer and the *New York Times*. And the team just exploded. Nine months in and I was running an engineering team that was thirty strong. It was my job to ensure we were always thinking up new plans and rolling them out. That meant guiding the team in a nonstop search for solutions to complex technical and organizational problems, while also making decisions about strategy and hiring new staff. And that was only the beginning. My job, like so many, was a daily balancing act between priorities, because everything—of course—had to happen at once.

In time I started to notice something: real progress doesn't come from doing the work you feel like doing or whatever springs to mind in the moment. The busier my job got, the more I realized I needed to find a whole new way to work.

Getting there took years of trial and error, but I'm glad to say my efforts paid off. I found my method. Along the way I devoured books like David Allen's *Getting Things Done* and Cal Newport's *Deep Work*. The books were big inspirations and taught me a lot. But knowing which tip to apply when? That's an art in itself. Without that, it's a little like being handed a bunch of screwdrivers, pliers, and hammers without knowing what the tools are for—let alone how or when to use them. Not at all surprising, then, that people tend to fall back on the familiar. That's happened to me more times that I can count. But I knew there had to be a better way, a smart approach to working that was flexible enough to accommodate day-to-day surprises. So I kept experimenting with my workweek.

Step by step, I arrived at my method, built from flexible and interlinking parts. The great thing about GRIP is that it doesn't just work for me. Friends and coworkers started trying it too. It was exciting to watch what it brought to their lives. In the last couple of years more and more people wanted to know about my method, so I decided to write it all down.

When this book came out in my native Dutch, it immediately hit the bestseller list. I was floored. Not a day goes by that I don't find notes from readers in my mailbox. Some write about their successes, but most talk about how happy they are to have finally found their own way of working: One that gives them clarity in the chaos. One that helps them deal with all the information and distractions bombarding us every day. And one that helps ensure they get their most important work done. Turns out loads of people have discovered, as I did, that a few simple building blocks, using tools you already know—a calendar, a to-do list, email—can make you loads more effective. With this English edition, I hope to share my method with everyone who's looking for a better grip on their jobs and their lives. That was always important, but the seismic shift in how we work since the pandemic hit in 2020 makes it even more apparent: our way of working could use some love and attention.

But first, a word of warning. One thing you won't hear me say on these pages is this: "*Take it easy. Stop working so hard.*" True, our busy lives mean we often pile too much on our plates. I'm all too familiar with pushing the limits and taking on too much—combining a demanding job with a toddler and a newborn, moving to a new home amidst it all, and finally transitioning away from Blendle to found a new startup. But in the following chapters I won't urge you to slow down or curb your ambitions. I want to help you be more intentional about the time you have and get more out of life, because I think we don't get that kind of encouragement nearly enough. And who doesn't want to lead a full life? The key is not to work even *harder*, but to do things *smarter* and make sure you get around to what really matters to you. That's why I start out in part 1 by showing you some practical ways to get a better grip on your days and get smarter and more strategic about how you spend your time.

START HERE!

1 GRIP AND YOUR WEEK

Get greater clarity and purpose using familiar tools in new ways.

- Calendar
- To-do list
- Email
- Friday recap

2 GRIP AND YOUR YEAR

Figure out what you want. Pick a path and learn to set goals you'll actually do.

- Setting goals
- Your Year Plan Day
- Accountability

3 GRIP AND YOUR LIFE

Hone the skills that shape your life, like listening, strategic thinking, and making big plans happen.

- Being yourself, but better
- Smart listening
- Solving issues
- Think big, start small

Part 2 starts with the question: What makes you want to get out of bed in the morning? We'll look at how to set goals you'll actually meet and how to make plans for the year to come. By getting to grips with the details, you'll free up space for bigger plans.

In the final part of the book I'll show you how to tap into your personal capabilities. Because how well do you truly know yourself? Are you a good listener? Do you know how to come up with smarter solutions? How to boost your self-image? Are you bold enough to think big, to dream up projects that could easily stretch five or ten years?

I know this sounds like a lot. As I said, I'm not going to tell you to do less. (I'll leave that to your friends or family.) What I will do is help you—and challenge you—to make smarter choices. To rethink how you go about your work. To take things up a notch at strategic moments, and how to choose what *not* to do. To set your own course, because if you don't take the lead, someone else will choose for you.

Before we get started, I have one last question: Are you the kind of person who likes life to be as *unstructured* as possible? Someone who thrives on freedom and working organically? I feel you. I've worked with plenty of people who share that outlook and were skeptical of my approach. But after trying it out, they became enthusiastic about this way of working. Why?

- By taking a slightly more structured approach to a few key aspects of your work, you can be *less structured* about the rest of your week. And *less stressed*.
- While the elements in this book are all interlinked, this method is by no means an all-or-nothing affair. You can start by trying out the tips for the biggest stressors (say, email) and build from there. Keep what works for you, ditch what doesn't.
- Some parts of this book can be addictive, because they're guaranteed to help you get more done and to do it better. That's worth a try, right?
- The whole idea behind this working method is that you're free to deviate from it, because there's a built-in safety net to

fall back on. The *Friday recap* is key in this regard. But more on that later, in chapter 4.

So are you ready? Time to dive in!

NEED A HAND?

I've created a free tool to go with this book. Sign up at gripbook.com/app and I'll help you jump-start applying what you read to your own workweek.

PART 1

GRIP

AND YOUR

WEEK

Whether you're a student or CEO, public servant or president, starting a new job or starting your own business, you have exactly seven twenty-four-hour days at your disposal each week. No more, no less.

Want to get more done with less hassle? Don't look at how much time you have. Look at how you spend it.

You'll make better use of the hours we all have if you pick a path and then spend time on what matters most. Picking a path—and sticking to it—sounds pretty straightforward. But with all the things life throws at you, it can be anything but. Not to worry. We're going to start simple, by defining exactly what that path is (your priorities) and planning out a single workweek.

In the first part of this book I'll show you how to work strategically. In practical terms, we'll look at how to get a better grip on the hours in your workweek. How you can use your calendar, to-do list, and email to get your work done faster and better. And how to handle all the unexpected stuff that comes your way.

Whenever people ask me for suggestions about how they work, my first question is always: "What's your schedule look like this week?" The answer tells me right off whether they have a plan for their week before they dive in. And whether they have a strategy. Now you might say: "Of course I put all my appointments on my calendar—tell me something I don't know!"

Challenge accepted.

1. YOUR CALENDAR IS YOUR ROCK

Setting priorities, scheduling your work, and making it happen

Your calendar is the basis of everything. Okay, glad we got that straight.

In a workweek where plans can change at any moment, you want one thing you can always rely on. Something solid you can look to when things get chaotic. Make that thing your calendar.

Much as I like trying out new tools, I always come back to my trusty calendar in the end. It has helped me tremendously over the years—not just to keep track of appointments, but to structure my workweek. In fact, it's the bedrock I build my week on. Whatever else happens, my calendar tells me what really matters. I spend less energy wondering, "What should I do first this morning?" because I can just check my calendar.

To make your calendar work for you, it has to be *up to date*. Want your calendar to be rock-solid reliable? Want to never again overlook a critical deadline or appointment? Then from now on, just do what your calendar says. Period. If you're scheduling time there for things you're not doing, now's the time to scrap those appointments. Be brutal. That recurring meeting you never attend? Cancel it. The old reminders for *bookkeeping* that you always ignore? Delete them.

Start fresh with only those items you know you'll stick to.

1. Your calendar is finite

Your calendar only has so much room, and that can feel limiting. Just think: if there were more hours in a day you could park your whole to-do list in your calendar. But a calendar's limits are actually its most brilliant feature. That's how it protects you from overextending yourself.

You probably already put important meetings and appointments on your calendar, but what about day-to-day work? Most people don't bother scheduling time for their own tasks. But when you add your *own work* to your calendar, it makes your true workload visible at a glance. You're less likely to pile too much on your plate because you know when it's full. That makes it much easier to say *no* when you need to.

More important, it's what empowers you to say: "Yes, I'd love to!" to that exciting new opportunity that comes up. Because you'll know you can fit it in.

2. Your calendar is like a navigation system

A navigation system does more than give you directions from A to B. Most will show you where traffic is backed up and guide you to the nearest gas station when you need one. All so you can keep your eyes on the road. That's convenient because you only need to keep track of one system, and one system keeps things simple, right?

I bet you also already use some kind of calendar. So why not take full advantage of everything this familiar tool can offer? No need for extra apps or add-ons. Your calendar will help get you where you want to go each week. And with less hassle.

3. Your calendar keeps track of how you spend time

By setting aside time in your calendar for your own tasks, you'll get used to figuring out how much time you need for those tasks beforehand. After all, it's hard to schedule time to do research for a new client, prepare a presentation, or draft a quote without first estimating whether you need half an hour or two. And when you finish a task, you'll know right away if your estimate was on the long or the short side. You've created a direct feedback loop that's going to help you plan more accurately. Another huge benefit: getting good at these estimates and delivering your work on time helps build trust with bosses, colleagues, and clients.

4. Your calendar is public

Most companies now let staff share their calendars so everybody can see when everybody else is available. If your employer does this, it's another excellent reason to schedule all your work for the week ahead. That way your coworkers and managers can see what you're working on, which is especially helpful when working remotely. But the biggest benefit of scheduling your work? Colleagues won't automatically assume you're free.

USING YOUR CALENDAR

Okay, enough theory: time for action! Now we're going to plan your week in six steps, blocking time for all the most important stuff. Not sure what those things are? Don't worry, we'll figure that out as we go.

Step 1. Choose a calendar

When choosing a calendar, go for the digital kind that you can access on all your devices (laptop, smartphone, office computer, tablet, or whatever else you use for your work). Pick one you like using.

A paper calendar may get the job done, but I'm not a fan and here's why. For starters, you miss out on loads of helpful features. A paper calendar won't send you reminders and you can't share it easily with other people. Plus plans tend to change, and that can be a pain on paper.

Personally, I like Google Calendar. But similar planning tools like Microsoft Outlook and Apple's iCloud work fine too. Go to gripbook.com/apps and I'll help you decide which calendar to use.

Step 2. Use your calendar for meetings of all kinds

The first thing to put in your calendar: plans you've made with other people for the coming week. You've probably done that already, but double-check just to be sure nothing's missing. If you're meeting off-site, you'll want to make sure you know where and include those details too.

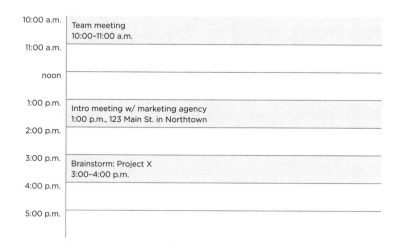

Step 3. Determine the stop time

A third detail you need to decide when planning an appointment is: What time will it end? In the next step I'll show why it's important to include specific stop times in your calendar, but for now just go ahead and make your best guess. If you know from experience that meetings with certain people tend to run over, factor that in too. The key is to be realistic.

Step 4. Send out invites to people

When I'm the one scheduling meetings, I try to make a point of sending out invites to everyone. Digital calendars let you do this easily by adding people's email addresses. That way they also have direct access to the meeting details. If it's a virtual meeting, don't forget to include the info people will need to join. Another reason I recommend sending out invites: it forces you to consider the length of your meeting. I've noticed it makes me more mindful of other people's time. Say I want to schedule coffee with a client to get acquainted. Clearly, two hours would be asking too much of their time. But what about one hour? Or

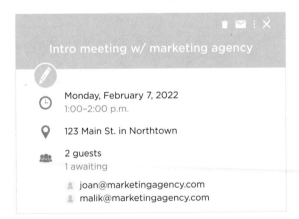

should I keep it to a short-and-sweet thirty minutes? By scheduling both a start and stop time in your calendar, you let others know what to expect. Sometimes I'll ask the other person to send me an invite. It's a gentle way of saying: "You decide how much time you have for me."

Step 5. Travel, prep, and postmeeting time

Don't forget to include time on the road. Travel can take up an important chunk of your schedule, yet it's easy to overlook. A simple way to avoid this pitfall is to make a habit of scheduling travel time when you plan an appointment.

Also, don't forget about prep time. Preparing for meetings is the easiest way to make your time together more effective. To figure out how much time you need, ask yourself: What will it take to make this meeting run smoothly? You can break it down using this checklist:

CHECKLIST

- How much time do I need to get to the meeting?
- How much time do I need to prepare?
- Can I prep on the day itself, or does it need to be earlier?
- Do I need to send any materials to people ahead of time?
- Is there anything I need to order or buy beforehand?
- Are there any meeting outcomes I can anticipate and plan for now? Should I go ahead and set aside time for those actions?

You can schedule time separately in your calendar for meeting prep, travel, and postmeeting tasks. In the example shown, I prepped for a meeting on the day itself. In most cases, that works fine. The result might look like this:

9:00 a.m.	
	Team meeting prep 9:30 a.m.
10:00 a.m.	Team meeting 10:00–11:00 a.m.
11:00 a.m.	Plan out actions from the team meeting 11:00 a.m.
noon	Travel Mytown—Northtown 12:00–1:00 p.m.
1:00 p.m.	Intro meeting w/ marketing agency 1:00 p.m., 123 Main St. in Northtown
2:00 p.m.	Travel Northtown—Mytown 2:00–3:00 p.m. / Brainstorm prep 2:30 p.m.
3:00 p.m.	Brainstorm: Project X 3:00–4:00 p.m.
4:00 p.m.	Brainstorm follow-up: plan actions and finalize minutes 4:00 p.m.
5:00 p.m.	

I can see right off that my day is blocked almost solid with three meetings, but that there's enough leeway to arrive prepared and on time, *and* to work through what was discussed in the team meeting and brainstorming session right afterward.

Step 6. Use your calendar for your own work

This last step is key: adding *your own work* to your calendar. Of course meetings are part of that, too, but here I want to focus on your most important day-to-day activities. Here's where your calendar can make all the difference.

Think for a second about how you spend money. Especially with big purchases, we tend to be critical, running down a mental checklist before deciding whether an expense is worth it. Somehow we're not nearly as careful with our time. Precious hours slip through our fingers like sand. So let's try a little thought experiment. I'd like you to think back to your last vacation. More specifically, to the week before you left.

That final week—before you switch on your out-of-office reply and shut down your computer for some much-deserved time off—feels different from other weeks. Why? Because you have a hard deadline and a clear picture of where you want to be at week's end. You're fueled by a healthy pressure because after that week your time's up. Your thinking gets black-and-white: What's critical? What's feasible, timewise? What's definitely not realistic? The fact that you have to set strict priorities tends to make a pre-vacation week the most productive and effective of all. (By the way, I've included a bonus chapter with tips for going on vacation.)

With this new approach to your calendar, you can make each week every bit as productive and effective. You're going to schedule work on your calendar based on the specific day and time that you need or want to do it. This approach forces you to weigh what you'll do in a given week (and what you definitely won't do). Remember what I said at the very beginning of this chapter: your calendar is your rock. Use it to make appointments with yourself. Whatever's on your calendar is what you're going to show up for. So, when deciding what to do this week, choose carefully!

To help me decide what goes on my calendar, I stick to a thirty-minute rule. Items go on it if they'll take me thirty minutes or more, or else are so urgent that I want to make sure I don't overlook them. And sure, there are loads of things I need to do that fall short of the thirty-minute rule. Those tasks get parked in my to-do list, which we'll get into in the next chapter.

So what goes on your calendar this week? This is where it gets tough. You may have no problem coming up with the broad strokes of what you want to accomplish this week. But when it comes to scheduling concrete tasks for Wednesday and Thursday morning, it's easy to feel overwhelmed. There's just so much to do. It's tempting to throw up your hands and do what seems best at the time. But if there's one thing that won't help you get the important work done, it's feeling your way through the week. Pushing yourself to start on that complex but crucial job rarely feels good, so odds are you'll focus instead on something that doesn't deserve your attention just then.

To help you finish every week with the same sense of satisfaction you have just before going on vacation, I've set out three selection filters below. (Too bad there's not a vacation at the end of each week to reward our efforts!)

CHOOSING YOUR TASKS

Filter 1. What are my priorities?

Once you know what your priorities are, deciding how best to invest your time gets far easier. It's a matter of filling in the blanks. You schedule blocks of time for each priority. Then decide what step comes next for each priority. When it's time for your appointment with yourself, you know which priority you're working on and can dive right in to work on a specific next step. Base your calendar on your priorities, and you'll be amazed how much you get done.

So how do you figure out what your priorities are? The best place to start is with your responsibilities. The following list can help you get a quick overview:

- Your job description or duties
- The objectives of your company, department, or team

- Priorities you've set with your manager
- Performance review feedback
- Recurring items in presentations or reports to your manager or team
- Major projects you're working on at the moment

Let's imagine you're the team leader of the corner coffeehouse. Using the list above, your responsibilities could look something like this:

- *Based on your location's new quarterly targets:* Responsible for growing daily sales by 3 percent
- *Based on your job description:* Responsible for a pleasant and dependable team of baristas
- *Based on your job description:* Final responsibility for the quality of products served
- *Based on your performance review:* Boost creative input in day-to-day activities and reduce staff turnover

These responsibilities determine your priorities. But before you can tackle them, you have to translate these priorities into specific tasks. Looking at each priority, what's the smallest first step you could take to make progress? As the coffeehouse team leader, you could:

- Review the latest monthly figures to find openings for growth
- Go through recent applications to see if there are any good candidates for the team
- Brainstorm creative ways to make the location stand out more

- Spend more one-on-one time with your team members to spot signs of dissatisfaction
- Plan a team outing and team meeting to boost employee morale and retention
- Schedule a talk with a prospective supplier about expanding your coffee bean range

Apart from these important tasks, your job as a team leader also involves the kind of routine work we're all familiar with:

- Your inbox has thirty-eight emails awaiting replies
- The kitchen fridge isn't closing properly and people are complaining
- Twice now, staff have come to tell you the milk is running low
- One employee didn't show up this morning and business has been nonstop today
- You were supposed to finalize next week's roster yesterday
- And so on

If you can think of dozens of actions like this for your job, rest assured: you're not alone. Maybe you even feel dazed by the sheer amount of jobs—big and small—awaiting you. That's completely understandable. The team leader in my example also has way too much on their plate. And while some of those things need to be addressed right away, one week clearly isn't enough to get through it all. (And remember, it's the week before that vacation!) That means we have to be choosy.

Fortunately, there's also a selection filter for this step: the Eisenhower Matrix.

To-do list

Are you feeling stressed out by all the unfinished tasks piling up in your head? Here's a quick fix. You can beat the feelings of chaos and regain peace of mind by grabbing a sheet of paper and writing down everything that's cluttering your thoughts right now. *All* the work you need to do, the people you need to see, and the things you need to follow up on. And by *all*, I really do mean *all*. Take your time. Get everything down. This may be just a temporary fix, but it's very effective all the same. You don't even have to cross anything off your list to feel clearheaded and calm about where you stand. In the next chapter we'll get to a more permanent solution to this stress: a to-do list.

Filter 2. Is there a good balance between urgency and importance?

President Dwight D. Eisenhower once said: "I have two kinds of problems, the urgent and the important. The urgent are not important, and the important are never urgent." The chart below visualizes this concept and provides a simple and brilliant tool to distinguish important tasks from urgent ones. The matrix has two axes. The vertical one represents a task's importance, from low to high, and the horizontal one represents its urgency.

These two axes form four quadrants into which a task can fall:

1. IMPORTANT and URGENT: These are important tasks that can't wait. Think urgent problems or projects with a strict deadline. To go back to our coffeehouse example: the employee who didn't show up for work leaves you with a very important and acute problem. If alarm bells are going off, it belongs in the first quadrant.

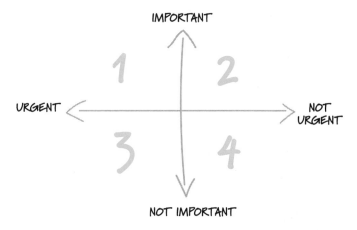

IMPORTANT

1   2

URGENT ← → NOT URGENT

3   4

NOT IMPORTANT

THE EISENHOWER MATRIX

2. IMPORTANT and NOT URGENT: Things in this quadrant can be postponed for a week or so without dire consequences. But you can't afford to put them off too long because these activities or projects will benefit you in the long run. Things that belong in this quadrant include planning a strategy, improving team processes, investing in customer relations, or investing in yourself. To use our coffeehouse example: the team leader was asked for more creative input at her latest performance review. This kind of goal will never feel urgent, but it's very important. A useful way to spot important and non-urgent tasks is to ask yourself: If I *don't* do this, will I run into problems down the road? If the answer is yes, then you're dealing with something that's important and not urgent. If the answer is no, then it's not important and not urgent.

3. URGENT and NOT IMPORTANT: This quadrant is about things that don't matter all that much over the long term, but are howling for attention this week. A coworker wants you to tweak a presentation at the last minute or—in our coffeehouse example—the milk's running low. With tasks in this quadrant, you have to consider whether they're genuinely urgent. Whenever other people want something from us, we tend to assume they're in a hurry, when often they may not mind waiting a day or even a week. I've noticed that in most cases it's perfectly fine to postpone this kind of stuff to a time that works better for me—as long as I let the other person know. Better yet, try to delegate or outsource things in this quadrant. If you're self-employed, that's not always an option. In that case, I recommend structuring your workday to minimize the impact of these kinds of urgent tasks, if necessary by scheduling some time every day for putting out fires. That way, your days won't get away from you when someone else has an emergency.

4. NOT URGENT and NOT IMPORTANT: This is the kind of work you want to avoid if at all possible, because it doesn't help you in any way. This category includes everything from constantly refreshing your inbox to meetings that don't go anywhere. I'm sure you can come up with plenty more examples of this kind of busywork: things you continue to do even though no one really benefits. For the occasional quick break these activities are fine, but often they're just a convenient excuse to put off more important work.

In general, we tend to do far too much work from the first quadrant—things that are important and urgent, like urgent projects with strict deadlines. And when we're not doing that kind of work, we're putting out fires in the third quadrant—fixing problems that are urgent but not important in the long run.

Even with these tools at my disposal, I still catch myself doing this all the time. Like recently, when I'd planned to work on ideas for the coming quarter. This was something important I needed to do that would fundamentally help the company move forward. But rather than buckling down, I chose to work on an upcoming email campaign instead. While that campaign was important, I definitely could have found a way to focus on the quarterly plan. I could have asked a coworker to take over the email campaign, for example, or consulted with the team to see if it was really essential to do the campaign right *now*.

Improving your decisions here is going to have a profound impact on your work. Here's a good way to see whether you're working on something truly important: Might the work help you qualify for a possible raise, promotion, or award? Or at least an honorable mention of some sort at the end of the year?

Impact

It's a word that gets thrown around a lot, but what does it actually mean? Often, *impact* just sounds like vague jargon. Where I talk about impact in this book, I mean things that genuinely help you, your team, or the company you work for. To know if what you're doing has impact, you have to know what's important. Which qualities matter? Which figures are key? At most commercial companies, that's sales and profits. At the news platform I worked for, we also closely tracked the number of articles read and number of subscribers, for instance. So if you want your work to have an impact, anything that boosts these figures is a good bet.

Let's turn back now to your list of work for the coming week. For every new item you add to this list, try to figure out where it falls in the Eisenhower Matrix. If you're the team leader at the coffee place and you think the quality of your coffee is already awesome, the impact of meeting with a potential new supplier probably won't be very high. That makes this a non-important and non-urgent activity and consequently not worth the time. If you're like me, you might feel inclined to do it anyway—after all, nothing ventured, nothing gained—but don't fall into this trap! If you want to get more important stuff done, you have to cut out everything that's not urgent and not important to you.

So, to recap: When drawing up your list of jobs for the week, think about how you could focus more of your energy on tasks in quadrant two (*important* and *not urgent*). If you can do that, you'll achieve impact. Next, take a critical look at things you've decided are *urgent* and *not important* to see if you can change tack or can pass them on to someone else. Anything that's *not important* and *not urgent* can be scrapped from your list. And while we're at it . . .

Filter 3. Am I focused enough?

After pinning down your responsibilities and rating your activities on urgency and importance, you might think you're good to go. But wait! We're not quite there yet. Pick up that red pen and let's run down your list for next week one more time. The thing is, humans are not natural-born planners. Even if you feel confident you'll get through your whole list next week, you likely still have too much on your plate. Luckily, there's a quick fix: shorten your list. Now's also the time to take another critical look at your scheduled meetings. Any chance they could get in the way of your main priorities?

How many jobs are on your list for the week? Thirty? Ten? Try whittling it down to two or three. I know, you'll feel the pain of saying no. But limiting how much you do lets you be honest about what's genuinely important. Even five big things to work on is still too many, so see if you can get it down to just two or three priority jobs this week. Starting small like this is an effective strategy for homing in on what matters most. And then if you finish those two or three and still have time left, you can always add more.

Let's put ourselves back in the shoes of that coffeehouse team leader one last time. Maybe you decide to spend this week on incoming job applications and organizing a day out for the team. By focusing on just these two tasks, you can be sure you'll make real progress.

Peter F. Drucker, the Austrian management guru, put it like this: "Develop your priorities and don't have more than two. I don't know anybody who can do three things at the same time and do them well. Do one task at a time or two tasks at a time. That's it." Because the thing is, if you set yourself five priorities, you really haven't prioritized at all.

FILLING IN YOUR CALENDAR

Now that you've done all the groundwork, it's finally time to fill in your calendar. And don't worry if it feels like a lot to take on board. If you follow these steps, then applying the three filters soon becomes second nature.

As you start scheduling your week, here are some pointers to keep in mind:

- Only block time for things that take thirty minutes or more. Anything less creates clutter. Put those shorter tasks on your to-do list. (We'll get to that in the next chapter.)

- Schedule as much time as you think you'll need. You don't want to rush yourself, but at the same time, don't set aside an hour for something you can do in half that.
- Take care not to schedule activities back-to-back and fill up your whole workday. If possible, leave about 20 percent of your working hours open. In an eight-hour workday, that's between ninety minutes and two hours. That leaves room for incidentals, breaks, and dealing with any urgent emails (more on that in chapter 3). It also builds in a buffer for the unexpected.
- I know keeping time free can feel like mission impossible, but give it a try—*especially* when you feel overextended. It will help you get those important things you have planned done. (If leaving time open results in extra meetings being planned for you, don't feel bad blocking off that time for yourself.)
- Describe items in a way that's clear to you. That way, when you glance at your calendar later this week you'll know exactly what to do. "Project plan" is pretty vague, but "Flesh out HQ renovation plans" instantly jogs your memory. Instead of wasting mental energy figuring out what to do, you can get straight to work.
- Choose the right time and place for each activity. Ask yourself: *Is this something I'd rather do in the morning? Do I need to be at the office to work on this? Are there people or resources I need?*

To give you an idea, here's what my week might look like.

	Monday	Tuesday	Wednesday
9:00 a.m.			Travel Mytown—Easttown 9:00–10:00 a.m.
	Team meeting prep 9:30 a.m.		
10:00 a.m.	Team meeting 10:00–11:00 a.m.	Market research 9:00 a.m.–12:00 pm	Appt w/ supplier X 10:00–11:00 a.m.
11:00 a.m.	Plan out actions from the team meeting 11:00 a.m.		Travel Easttown—Mytown 11:00 a.m.–12:00 p.m.
noon	Travel Mytown—Northtown 12:00–1:00 p.m.	Lunch 12:00 p.m.	
1:00 p.m.	Intro meeting w/ marketing agency 1:00 p.m., 123 Main St. in Northtown	1:1 w/ manager, 1:00 p.m.	
2:00 p.m.	Travel Northtown—Mytown 2:00–3:00 p.m. | Brainstorm prep		Brainstorm prep 2:30 p.m.
3:00 p.m.	Brainstorm: Project X 3:00–4:00 p.m.	Coffee w/ Sophia 3:30 p.m.	Brainstorm session on XYZ 3:00–4:00 p.m.
4:00 p.m.	Brainstorm follow-up: plan actions and finalize minutes 4:00 p.m.	Update admin 4:00–5:00 p.m.	
5:00 p.m.			

	Thursday	Friday
9:00 a.m.		Interview job applicant
10:00 a.m.		
11:00 a.m.		New team meeting 11:30 a.m.
noon		Lunch 12:00 p.m.
1:00 p.m.	All-day seminar 9:00 a.m.–5:00 p.m.	Project progress + report 12:30–1:30 p.m.
2:00 p.m.		Email 2:00–3:00 p.m.
3:00 p.m.		
4:00 p.m.		
5:00 p.m.		Office drinks 5:00–6:00 p.m.
6:00 p.m.		

On the face of it, it looks like I've been methodical about planning my week. I've included all my appointments and meetings and set aside some chunks of time for key tasks. My three main priorities are also clear: market research on Tuesday morning, a brainstorming session on Wednesday afternoon, and an all-day course on Thursday. Even so, there are some things I've overlooked.

1. On Monday I've blocked time to prepare for meetings, but what about my meetings on other days? Looks like I don't have any prep time before seeing my manager on Tuesday or the interview and two in-house meetings on Friday.

2. Do I have what I need to dive into my market research on Tuesday morning? And do I really need three whole hours?

3. Am I meeting Sophia on Tuesday afternoon at the office, or do I need to travel somewhere? Realistically, will I be back in time to tackle admin at 4:00 p.m.?

4. Is there anything I need to do ahead of my Wednesday meeting with the supplier?

5. On Thursday I have an all-day seminar. Is there any homework I still need to do from last time? And where will the class be held?

6. Do I need to read up on the candidate I'm interviewing on Friday? Do I have my questions lined up? Am I doing the interview alone or with the team?

7. Is one hour really enough to get through all my emails, or will I need more time? (We'll get to email in chapter 3.)

Taking a critical look at your calendar before the week starts is going to make all the difference between struggling to keep up all week and staying on top of things. Essentially, you'll be tackling each new task under the best possible conditions. You'll be amazed how quickly you get up to speed at doing this. To help you get started, here are some more insights that come in handy for me.

1. Mixing creative and non-creative work is taxing

It was an essay by Paul Graham that opened my eyes to the fundamental difference between "managers" and "makers."[1] Graham—known in the startup world as the founder of Y Combinator and an investor in the likes of Airbnb and Dropbox— talks about how much effort it takes makers to continually shift back and forth between meetings and work. Managers carve their days into hours, or even half hours, and are used to switching between tasks all the time. But those quick switches don't work as well for makers like writers or programmers. Makers need longer stretches of time to do their thing because it's tough, if not impossible, to make solid progress on a text or a tricky section of code in just an hour. As Graham points out, creatives work best in blocks of whole or half days. A single thirty-minute interruption can wreck their productivity. So does that mean a workplace with both types of schedules can't function? Not at all, according to Graham. Problems only arise when the two schedules meet.

My own approach is more "manager" than "maker." I'm constantly shuttling between tasks. But I've also learned to routinely build in big blocks of time to get creative work done, like thinking about my company's future. I need to combine both schedules, setting aside whole or half days for tasks that entail creative thought, while filling at least half my week with meetings that take an hour or less. Since realizing that these two kinds of work take different kinds of concentration and different kinds of planning, I'm able to get a lot more done with less effort. It's also made me more mindful about disrupting other peoples' schedules. If they're in maker mode, a meeting with me could be a big drain on their productivity. Fortunately, there's a simple solution: Just pick a time when interruptions are less problematic, like around lunchtime or at the end of the day. Or if you can check the other person's calendar, try to schedule it right before or after their other meetings, without breaks.

2. Your new calendar will take some getting used to

If your scheduling philosophy up until now was, "Here's what I'm hoping to do this week; if it doesn't work out, there's always next week," then the approach I'm suggesting will be a radical change. Give it some time. Try, meanwhile, to stay true to your new motto—*my calendar is my rock*—and also schedule yourself some extra breathing room at first. Again, it's better to strike items from your calendar than fail to stick to it. Planning your weeks will soon grow on you, as you start to experience the ease this approach brings to your days.

3. Do important stuff first

We have only so much time and energy to spend in a day. After channeling our energy into doing what we're "supposed to" all day, we tend to ease up toward evening.

Brian Tracy writes about this in his book *Eat That Frog.* He borrowed the title from a line attributed to Nicolas Chamfort: "Eat a live frog first thing in the morning and nothing worse will happen to you the rest of the day." In other words, start with your least favorite, most aggravating task, instead of putting it off all day.

Stephen Covey developed a whole principle around this idea, which he calls *First Things First*. He uses a brilliant metaphor to explain: Imagine you want to fill a glass with both as many rocks and as much sand as possible. The rocks represent your big, important work, while the sand is all the other stuff you also need to do. If you fill your glass with sand first and then try to put in the rocks, you'll have a lot more rocks left over than if you'd put the rocks in first and then the sand.

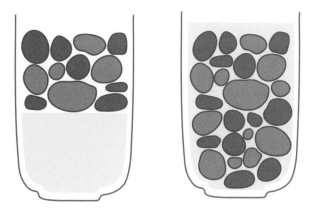

You'll get more of the big stuff in your life done if you schedule it sooner rather than later—early in the week, early in the day. Make it a habit. There's no simpler way to get more important work done than by consistently prioritizing it in your calendar. The American statesman Benjamin Franklin had a similar strategy. Every morning, he asked himself the same question: "What good shall I do today?" That's a great way to kick-start your workday.

4. You're not a machine

For a long time, I was set on doing important creative work on Thursday and Friday afternoons. Through sheer force of will, I could do well at whatever I wanted whenever I wanted. Or so I thought. Until I adopted a rhythm that actually suited me. As soon as I shifted creative time to the beginning of my week—especially mornings—the quality of my work took off. I also realized that sometimes I do my best brainwork alone in the office after everyone's gone home, or at my kitchen table.

The lesson? We're not machines. We do different types of work better at different times in different places. Once you figure out which tasks you do best when, you'll not only be more effective but also enjoy your work more. Instead of fighting against the current, you're buoyed by it.

At my old company, Blendle, we came up with a policy we called *meet-free Tuesdays*. After the weekly round of Monday meetings, everyone was on the same page and ready to go. On Tuesdays we harnessed that energy, keeping our schedules clear so we could all make some serious headway on our own work.

5. Treat your calendar like a fitness regimen

We all know that strength training helps build muscles. You can up your focus and concentration with some training too. The more often and longer you concentrate, the better at it you'll be. Here's where your calendar comes in. It lets you schedule time for concentrated work, a little more each week. Start with small blocks of time and build it out slowly—just like a fitness plan.

Scheduling your whole week has an added bonus: You don't have to keep shifting back and forth between planning your work and actually doing it. When it's time to get started on something, you can dive right in. And if you get interrupted or distracted, just check your calendar to get back on track.

Back in 1908, Arnold Bennett wrote a book called *How to Live on 24 Hours a Day*. In it, he lays out a great concentration exercise. On your way to work, he says, try to think about only one thing: "When you leave your house, concentrate your mind on a subject (no matter what, to begin with). You will not have gone ten yards before your mind has skipped away under your very eyes and is larking round the corner with another subject." We all know how much our minds like to wander. Bennett did, too, and his method from over a hundred years ago has a lot in common with the meditation and mindfulness people practice today. Bennett encourages us to train our brains, and to understand that it *is* possible to improve concentration and direct our thoughts.

DEALING WITH THE UNEXPECTED

If you could map out every detail of your week ahead of time, life would get dull fast. But lucky for us, life is unpredictable. Good thing, because creativity thrives on surprises. And great ideas often strike when you least expect them. When it comes to your workweek, however, surprises are mostly inconvenient or problematic. Then again, if your schedule leaves plenty of time to respond to curveballs without breaking a sweat, you're probably not making the most of your workdays.

The first thing to do when dealing with unexpected interruptions is to start guarding your work schedule like a terrier. That takes some practice. And no one's going to guard your calendar for you; it's up to you. Once you've carefully set priorities, coordinated with others, and decided where best to invest your energy, anyone who wants to interrupt your plans better have a good reason!

Headphone rule

At Blendle we had a headphone policy. Wearing headphones was like a *Do not disturb* sign. It meant you were in concentration mode and didn't want to be interrupted. It's too bad it took headphones to get the message across, but it worked like a charm.

Being firm and communicating clearly about when interruptions are okay and when they aren't can help you preserve your focus. That said, unexpected tasks are sure to come up. And sometimes you can't afford to put them off. When that happens, you might think a meticulously planned schedule would stand in your way, but it turns out the opposite is true. Your careful planning will help you deal handily with these situations as they arise—without losing your cool.

To see how, let's take another look at that workday I'd planned. Imagine this is your day. It's 11:40 a.m. You had a good meeting with the team and the morning went smoothly. You've scheduled action items from the meeting as planned, and now you're catching up on some emails before heading off to Northtown. Suddenly, your boss comes into your office with a job that needs to be done by the end of the day. You discuss it and realize you'll have to clear the rest of your afternoon to do it. Fortunately, your calendar tells you exactly what work you need to put on hold and what meetings to reschedule.

9:00 a.m.		
	Team meeting prep 9:30 a.m.	
10:00 a.m.	Team meeting 10:00-11:00 a.m.	
11:00 a.m.	Plan out actions from the team meeting 11:00 a.m.	
Noon	Travel Mytown—Northtown 12:00-1:00 p.m.	
1:00 p.m.	Intro meeting w/ marketing agency 1:00 p.m., 123 Main St. in Northtown	
2:00 p.m.	Travel Northtown—Mytown 2:00-3:00 p.m.	Brainstorm prep 2:30 p.m.
3:00 p.m.	Brainstorm: Project X 3:00-4:00 p.m.	
4:00 p.m.	Brainstorm follow-up: plan actions and finalize minutes 4:00 p.m.	
5:00 p.m.		

Your calendar can be a lifesaver at times like this, so you want to start reaching for it reflexively. In this case, you have to decide in minutes whether to keep your appointment in Northtown. The trip there and back for a meeting will take a big chunk out of your afternoon. Rescheduling feels awkward, but when you call the agency, it turns out they don't mind at all. Brainstorming Project X is important, too, but bumping it to another day isn't the end of the world. So, instead of trying to juggle everything—resulting in a rushed meeting with the research agency, a brainstorming session you can't focus on, and an evening of overtime—make a simple phone call to Northtown and send an email to the project team. That's all it takes to free up your afternoon for the work at hand.

1. Does the job really need to be done right now? Does it outweigh everything else you're doing? If not, schedule it for a better time.

2. How much time do you need to finish the job? Make a generous estimate and block that in your calendar.

3. Check your calendar for any conflicting items and see if you can reschedule. Don't worry yet about arranging a new date for that meeting with six colleagues, because right now you're in crisis mode and don't have a moment to spare. Just let them know you'll need to reschedule and set a reminder to come back to it later. As long as you explain the situation, people will understand.

Getting unexpected work at the last minute is frustrating when it upends your plans. At the same time, knowing exactly what you'll have to put on hold gives you clarity and peace of mind. And it allows you to adapt with ease. Worried you'll lose sight of postponed work? Don't be. The Friday recap, which we'll get to in chapter 4, creates a safety net under your week. Just let people know what you can't get around to today, and your Friday recap will put it back on your radar.

EXPERIMENT WITH YOUR WORKWEEK

Elite athletes go over every aspect of their lives, in search of anything that could boost their performance. From training techniques to details of diet, nothing goes unexamined. And when results don't measure up, the question is always, *What can I do differently next time?* Top athletes know: to change how you do, you have to change what you're doing.

You can use the same approach for work. With everything a job throws our way, it's safe to say we're already performing like athletes. So how to up your game? Experiment! Tweak your techniques and see if you like the effect.

Say you tend to stall out on Thursdays and have trouble sticking to your work plans. You could try working somewhere else that day—even sitting in a different room or facing another direction could do the trick. Anytime you have a sense you could do better, try changing your routine to see what helps. I've put together a list of questions to get you going:

Work vs. downtime

- After meetings, how long does it take you to get back into the flow of your work?
- How much breathing room do you need in your daily schedule to have a productive day?

Working early vs. late

- Do you do your best work in the mornings? Or does inspiration tend to strike late in the afternoon or evening?

Working in a busy vs. a quiet setting

- Do you work better with other people around? Or when you're alone?

Working with or without deadlines

- Do you thrive under pressure? When do you get better results: after several days of intense work with a deadline looming, or when you know you have all the time in the world?
- Is it easier or harder to stay focused if you know you have an appointment in two hours? Or that your laptop battery has about ninety minutes of juice left? Or that your toddler will be waking up within the hour?

Working earlier vs. later in the week

- Do you work better at the start of the workweek (after a restful weekend) or does it take until Thursday or Friday to hit your stride? How do your Mondays compare to your Fridays?

Routine vs. spontaneity

- Do you work better if your days follow a consistent pattern? Or do you get more and better work done on days with variation and room for spontaneity?

Working with or without music

- Do you work better with music, or do you find it distracting? What kind of music works well for you and what doesn't?

Grouped vs. individual tasks

- Do you get more done if you save up similar tasks and then tackle them all at once—like emailing, writing proposals, or organizing meetings—or does it make you anxious to see the work piling up?

Working standing up vs. sitting down

- Can you stay focused longer if you work standing up? Or does it wear you out?

Long workday or short

- Do you get more done if you work longer hours? Or do long workdays undermine the quality and/or quantity of what you do?

Working online or off

- Are you more productive with an active internet connection, or if you temporarily disconnect?

More vs. less sleep

- How does adding or losing an hour's sleep impact your productivity? Do you get a fresher start with or without an alarm clock?

Working together vs. on your own

- Do you get more done and have more ideas if you work in a team? Or do you work better solo?

Long lunch or short

- How long can you concentrate after your lunch break? Which works better: a short or a long break? Does it help to get some fresh air?

YOUR CALENDAR IS STAGE 1

Congratulations! You've lined up your priorities and planned out your calendar. All that's left is to do the work. And of course to enjoy the sense of getting to grips with your week. Instead of feeling swamped by everything you need to do, you've now put it into a clear framework.

If you're anything like me, you'll notice as the week goes by that you've blocked too little time for some things and too much for others. Or you may see just how often you get sidetracked by work you hadn't counted on. These observations are valuable, so it's worth jotting them down (see the box on Notes). Taking a moment to reflect on your week also helps you pick out recurring patterns in your work. Doing what's on your calendar gives you a better understanding of your week, and that in turn helps you plan the next one. It's a virtuous cycle.

Okay, so at this point you may be wondering: *Do I have to plan every week in all this detail? And how do I combine that with the other important parts of my job?* Don't worry. In the next chapters I'll walk you through the rest of your week. Anytime you need to figure out what to tackle next, just stick to *the three-stage rocket.*

Notes

You can make notes all kinds of ways, from jotting them down in a notebook or writing them on Post-its to using a digital system. You can probably guess that digital gets my vote. That way, I have quick and easy access across all my devices. Whatever method you choose, the most important thing is having a system you can rely on. Check the bonus chapter at the end of this book for more note-taking tips.

What I like about the three-stage rocket is it tells you what you should be doing at any given moment. Here's how:

- Whatever's on your calendar comes first. That's where you plan your work for the week and that's stage 1. Do what you have planned, because your calendar is your rock.
- Nothing else scheduled for the moment? Then you're ready for stage 2: things on your to-do list.
- No more to-dos set for today? Time for stage 3: emailing.

Now that you've got your calendar sorted, it's time to really take off. Stage 2 will give you what's perhaps the quickest win of the book: your very own backup brain.

THE 3-STAGE ROCKET

2. STOP STORING THINGS IN YOUR HEAD

Reclaim your brain with a smart to-do list

Do you ever finish your workday feeling more stressed than when you started? That evening, your mind's buzzing with all the things that still need doing.

Or maybe you're working on something that requires absolute focus, but random to-dos keep popping into your head. Reminders like "I still need to put in that vacation request," or "I've got to get back to so-and-so about that report."

Any task—large or small—that your brain keeps reminding you about can be seen as an *open loop*. And an open loop is a line that needs to be closed. Lines like this are useful because your work isn't done and your brain is hardwired to get you to do it. That means your brain reminds you of the open loop every chance it gets, hoping that at some point you'll do something about it.

There's just one problem with this mechanism: our brains have terrible timing. So you don't remember that ingredient you needed from the store until you unpack your groceries at home. Or the urgent question you had to ask a coworker pops into your head right *after* your weekly meeting. Because your brain is incapable of sending reminders at the right time, it ends up going into stalker mode, sending signals at random for as long as it takes you to finish a task. The more open loops, the more signals—and the more stress.

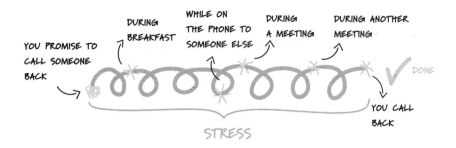

Psychologists group our daily thought processes in two basic systems: system 1 and system 2. This theory of *system thinking* was popularized by Daniel Kahneman in his bestseller *Thinking, Fast and Slow.*

System 1 thinking is fast, instinctive, emotional, and unconscious. It lets you do things like pinpoint the source of a sound, or add up 2 + 2, or cruise along the freeway (once you're an experienced driver).

System 2 is the exact opposite. It's slow, rational, deliberate, and conscious. Reversing your car into a parking space, giving a speech, or mapping a route from A to B are typical system 2 activities you can't do unconsciously. They force your brain to do active work, which it doesn't like. Your brain reacts by tempting you with easier work. After all, thinking about that leaky faucet that needs fixing takes less energy than concentrating on that complicated proposal you're trying to write. Try this: Take a second to look up from this book at the space you're in now. Chances are some totally unrelated task will spring to mind.

That's a relief because for a moment you don't have to digest the words on this page. That's how open loops disrupt our concentration, cause stress, and keep us from getting our work done.

How awesome would it be if we could temporarily block those open loops? If we could somehow take those reminders in our heads and put them on pause until the exact date, time, and place we *want* to be reminded? Maybe it will happen one day, but for now we don't have that kind of control over our brains.

The good news is there's another fix for open loops and the stress they can cause. The moment your brain is 100 percent sure that someone or something will remind you of a task, it turns down the volume on those persistent internal reminders. So what we really need is a *backup brain* just for reminders, to give our regular brain a break. Like an external hard drive for your mind.

Once you're no longer using your "working memory" for storage, that frees up your brain for the job at hand. Transferring all those open loops from our heads to this backup brain (or *second brain*) lets us focus fully on work that really matters. This brilliant insight and the idea for a smart to-do list comes from David Allen's powerful book *Getting Things Done.* As he puts it, "Your brain is a thinking machine, not a storage device."

That doesn't have to be complicated. If you stick to two basic practices, you'll keep your brain happy and your head clear:

- Move all open loops to your backup brain—the sooner the better
- Check in regularly with your backup brain

Neglect either one of these, and you'll feel the fog roll in. Your brain will go back to pestering you about every open loop and you'll wind up back where you started: stressed and overloaded. Sadly, we can't just dump our open loops in a backup brain and call it a day. We need to check in with our backup brain from time to time and keep it updated.

But as I said, it doesn't need to be complicated. The more straightforward, the more likely it will work. In his book *The Organized Mind*, neuroscientist Daniel Levitin points out that the share of people who like using a new organization system is inversely proportional to that system's complexity. That is, the simpler a system, the better our chances of sticking with it. The old law of diminishing returns also applies: your initial investment in the basics of a new system yields far more than all the subtle tweaks you make later.

YOUR BACKUP BRAIN

I love the idea of a backup brain. Who wouldn't want one? In the next few pages I'll show you how to build your very own external memory, one step at a time.

Your backup brain will actually consist of two parts. One is your calendar, which we've covered already. The other is a to-do list. The great thing about to-do lists, even in their simplest form, is they give you a place outside your head to park all your open loops, big or small. So, before we start building, make one solemn promise to yourself. It's the golden rule for using a to-do list:

Stop storing things in your head.

That's it!

You build your to-do list one step at a time. I've broken it down into six steps or *levels*. Each one takes you to the next. What's nice about this setup is the first few steps are both the easiest to do and have the biggest benefits.

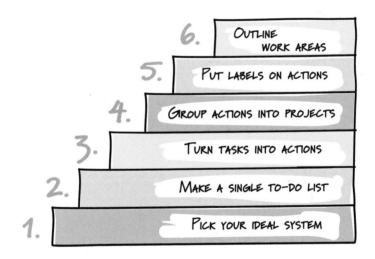

Level 1. Pick your ideal system

The first step is to pick a good system for your to-do list. You want an external backup that helps you focus better and reduce stress. *What system should I use?* is something I get asked a lot. But before I share my own favorites, here's what I mean by a good system:

- *It's digital.* To-do lists, like calendars, tend to get messy on paper. With tasks and priorities shifting all the time, using paper can lead to endless rewriting. A digital memory makes life a whole lot easier.
- *You can sync it on your phone and computer.* You're going to want quick access to your to-do list no matter where you are. That narrows the options considerably.
- *It's clear and fast.* So often, I see people struggling with sluggish systems or with software that creates more clutter than clarity. Go ahead and be picky. You want something you'll enjoy using.

Okay, now I'm going to make the choice a little easier for you. Got a Mac and an iPhone? Then I recommend Things (https://culturedcode.com/things/). Things is a super-speedy app for Mac and iPhone that's beautifully designed with loads of attention to detail.

If you use Windows and an Android phone, try out Todoist (https://todoist.com/). Todoist is clear and straightforward and works on all platforms.

Things is a paid app—and worth every penny—but you can try it free for fifteen days. Todoist has a free version with all the functionality you're likely to need. By the time you read this there may be better apps on the market, so check for my latest tips at gripbook.com/apps.

The last couple of years, I've noticed that more people I know are willing to pay for their software. I'm all for that because the difference between free and paid software can be huge. Think of it like a well-made tool. A carpenter would never skimp on tools because they know that better materials mean a better result. Better software can do the same for your work. And it can change your whole approach to to-do lists.

Found an app and installed it on your devices? Excellent. Let's move on to Level 2.

Level 2. Make a single to-do list

Whatever software you choose, at this stage it's easy to feel overwhelmed. You can create projects, tags, checklists, and add locations, attachments, colors, and notes—there are loads of options. And that's exactly why people tend to give up on this kind of system. Understanding the options and keeping track of it all is just too much.

I recommend you keep things as simple as possible. Start out with a single list. Hold off on the project lists and sublists for now. There's also no need to decide what you have to do today or at some point down the road. For most people, going from no list at all to one big digital list has by far the greatest benefits. So I'll say it again: start with a single list.

Most task-tracking software has a standard list labeled *inbox*. Look for it. Don't have it? Then create one. It's no accident this sounds like email, because it's a box for all your incoming messages. Only this inbox isn't for stuff sent by *other people*, but a catch-all for your own unorganized tasks. This task inbox is where you park all your open loops—all those things you keep telling yourself you need to do. And not only for work, but stuff to do with your house, vacation, hobbies, family—you name it. There are no rules dictating what you can or can't put in this inbox. Your only goal at this point is to get down literally everything that's in your head. How you describe tasks doesn't matter at this stage. Neither does scheduling. We'll get around to linking your to-do list and calendar later in the book, in chapter 4. Don't worry about double entries either. The only thing that matters now is that you've got all your tasks down somewhere in your system.

To give you an idea, here are some tasks in my inbox at the moment:

- Propose new setup for Monday meetings
- Make appointment w/ Makayla
- Report iOS app error to team
- Schedule road map session next week w/ Alex, Noor, and Ayden
- Buy trash bags

You can see my list throws a whole mix of work and personal tasks together. Some items are bigger and more important than others. Some are more pressing, others less so. That's not a problem. For now, just taking all these tasks out of your head and putting them into an external system helps tremendously.

If you're not used to this approach, it's easy to think: *Oh, I can easily remember this or that. No need to write it down.* But it's worth fighting that instinct and teaching yourself this new habit.

Once you get the hang of wrangling each task and open loop into this system, there's no going back. It's incredibly freeing.

This is also a great time to round up any old to-do lists you have lying around (scribbled on notepads, Post-its or paper napkins, or in a file of some sort on your phone or laptop) and add them all to your new inbox.

The checklist below can also be handy. It helps jog your memory for any other tasks you may have overlooked. There's always something. Remember, right now it doesn't matter if your list is useful; the goal is just to get down everything that pops into your head. So grab anything that hints at a task and throw it in your inbox—along with whatever else is on your mind.

CHECKLIST TO COMPLETE YOUR TO-DO LIST

- Ongoing projects
- Projects you want to start
- Goals you've set or that have been set for you (Like feedback from performance reviews. You looked at this already when filling in your calendar, but it makes sense to put goals and responsibilities on your to-do list too. This list looks beyond next week.)
- Clients
- Meetings you need to prepare for
- Appointments you need to make
- Presentations
- Important phone calls, voice mails, texts
- Important emails
- Budgets
- Paperwork
- Taxes
- Devices/equipment
- Personal development
- Stuff you want to read (books, journals, newsletters)
- Odd jobs around the house
- Things to be cleaned up

- Things you need to buy
- Hobbies
- Backups
- Important documents (order passport, renew driver's license)
- Places you need to go

MAKE IT QUICK

I was answering emails on my laptop the other day, when I suddenly remembered I had to find a repairman to fix something at the house. Without stopping to think (Daniel Kahneman's *fast thinking!*) I used a keyboard shortcut, typed "Take damage pics and get repair quote," and hit enter. In a matter of seconds, I could forget all about the repairman and go back to what I was doing. Quick access to your to-do list is essential. It will save you tons of time every day and preserve your focus. Go ahead and set one up now.

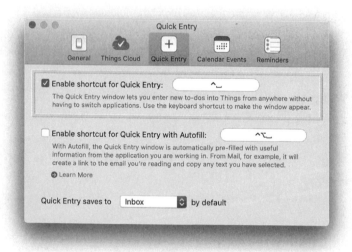

So how do you create a keyboard shortcut? If you're a Mac user and picked Things for your to-do list, you can use the *Quick Entry* option (click the menu in Things and then select Preferences). Pick a key combination you can type one-handed with ease, and start using it as much as you can so it becomes second nature.

Using your new software, you're taking all the chaos of unrelated reminders in your head and creating an orderly list. Now keep feeding your backup brain, in line with Practice 1: move any open loops to your backup brain as soon as you can.

Practice 2 was to check in regularly with your backup brain. Here's where the three-stage rocket (p. 38) comes in. Whenever you have a gap in your schedule, get used to reaching for your to-do list. Once you have it in front of you, take a moment to decide: What item moves things forward the most *and* is doable in the time you have right now? (Skip emails for the time being; we'll get to those in the next chapter.)

Once you start to work with your to-do list this way, you'll soon notice a greater sense of calm and clarity. And far less clutter in your head. But that's just the beginning: time for Level 3.

Level 3. Turn tasks into actions

How you describe tasks in your inbox makes a big difference in how much you get done. Get it right, and you'll be able to clear away work you've been putting off for ages, just because you've framed the action so it sounds simple and doable. How? Let's say you just attended a virtual leadership conference. When employees attend events like this, your company expects people to share lessons learned with the whole team, but leaves you free to choose how. As you're about to close your laptop on Friday evening after an exhausting week, your mind buzzing with new ideas, you remember this and add a task to your inbox:

- Share leadership conference lessons

Once you've taken this thought out of your head, you can relax over the weekend. You don't have any open loops to worry about.

Fast-forward to Monday morning. You have an empty slot on your calendar and see this task in your to-do list. Are you motivated to do it? Nah. Do you even know where to start? Not really. And that's mostly because of how it's worded. I mean, what's even the first step for this task? You can't get started if you still need to figure out what to do.

Now imagine that when you set yourself this task on Friday you worded it as a set of actions, like this:

- Type up conference notes
- Make ten slides on main conference lessons
- Send lunch presentation invites to team

These actions all sound doable, making them far more inviting to dive into. And the only difference is how you described the task. In the second example you know exactly what to do, putting the results within easy reach.

So if you feel stumped when you look at your to-do list, try turning your tasks into actions. Tasks tend to be vague, half-formed, too big, and fuzzy on the details. They serve a purpose, but lack spark. Actions have a verb. They energize and point you in the right direction. They're clear-cut and doable. If a task doesn't have a verb, that's a good clue it should be turned into one or more actions. The way I approach this is to ask myself a basic question when I add a task to my inbox. *If I wanted to tackle the task right now, does this tell me how?* To show you what I mean, here's how I turned some tasks into actions:

Turn **TASKS** that are too vague . . .	. . . into **ACTIONS** that are instantly doable.
REPORT ON PROJECT X	Ask Ben in Sales for input on Project X report
SET UP MARKETING CAMPAIGN	Schedule meeting w/ marketing agency (This works, but it would be smarter to prepare first, so→)
	Schedule meeting with Sarah re: marketing campaign (This works, but it would be better to come up with proposals and get some feedback first, so→)
	Draft proposal w/ 5 ideas for marketing campaign
	Discuss proposal with Hannah
TRIP PICS	Send trip pics for printing (This doesn't work, because there are just far too many photos, so→)
	Pick trip pics to print (This works, but they need to be edited first, so→)
	Edit trip pics (This works, but the photos aren't on my laptop yet, so→)
	Import camera pics
LEAKY GUTTER	Call someone to fix the gutter (This works, but need to find someone first, so→)
	Ask neighbor who she called in last week to do the repairs on her place

By taking just a little more time to formulate them, you can upgrade vague tasks into concrete actions you'll actually do. Actions give you a handle on what you need to do first and how much time you need to do it, so starting a new task takes less energy. Lao Tzu hit on this over 2,500 years ago when he said: "Even a journey of a thousand miles begins with a single step." While carving empty directives into clear-cut actions can feel like you're spinning your wheels, it's what gives your plans traction. It's the single most effective way to ease into taking that first step. And the next one. And the next.

If I can't come up with an action for a task right away, I do the next best thing and make a note in my inbox: *Figure out next action for Project X.* That way I've at least created a follow-up action for myself that tells me exactly what I need to do.

There's just one more thing before we move on to the next level. Part of making tasks *actionable* is to add a date. But unlike tasks you put in your calendar that have to happen within a narrow window, the dates you assign to actions on your to-do list are just a *guide.* They mean you'd like to do the action on or around that date. The reason for being specific is pure portion control. It limits how many actions you set for a day while also decluttering your inbox. As soon as you assign a date to an action, it disappears from your inbox. You're left with only those tasks you still have to deal with.

Giving tasks a provisional date also does something else. It makes the question *What should I start on next?* much easier to answer. You no longer have to weigh all the items on your big list, but can dive into your to-dos for that day.

I've made Level 2 (p. 45) and Level 3 (p. 49) separate steps here. But with a little practice, wording tasks as actions will come naturally. And the more you experience the rewards of making your to-dos actionable from the outset, the less you'll have to bother with Level 2.

Once you've mastered your task inbox, you're ready for the next step: How do you keep sight of the big picture amid all those tasks? The answer is *projects*: by grouping a set of actions together under one heading.

Level 4. Group actions into projects

So you've moved all the tasks that were floating around in your head to an external to-do list. And you've translated them all into clear-cut actions. Good job. You're now one of the happy few walking around with a clear head. But there will likely come a day when your to-do list starts running wild. Happens to the best of us. Dozens of tasks pile up in your inbox. That's a good time to think about creating a clearer breakdown for your tasks. Over the next couple of pages, I'll show you how to group that long list of random tasks into a handful of workable projects.

THE *SOMEDAY* PROJECT

Let's start simple. In Level 2 you parked a whole variety of tasks—big and small—in your task inbox. But there's no way you can do them all this minute. That's no problem. Time to create your first project in your new software. I like to call this project *Someday*. This is a place where you can drop all the ideas you don't have time for right now (and maybe not for a few weeks or even months). They're ideas for some point in the future. A professional course you're thinking about taking, new opportunities for next quarter, cleaning out the garage, scanning old vacation pictures, or the sabbatical you want to take in a few years.

Separating short-term from long-term tasks cleans up your to-do list. You don't have to keep scrolling through tasks that aren't relevant right now, but you do have them all filed away.

The image below is my sample Someday project. Adding a Someday project is a great way to declutter your to-do list. (A Someday project comes standard in the Things app.) So go ahead and scan your inbox. You're sure to find some tasks and actions you won't get around to for several weeks. Drag them to your Someday project. If you're worried you'll forget about them, don't be. In the next chapter I'll show you how to keep track of these tasks and actions.

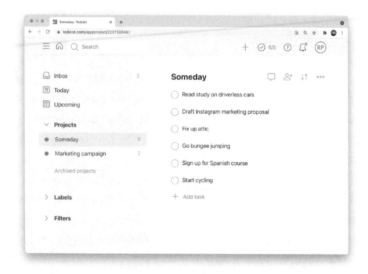

It's worth stressing again that the greatest value of a to-do list is that it gets tasks out of your head and into an external digital system. And remember: the more complicated you make your backup brain, the less likely you are to keep using it. I've seen people enthusiastically start grouping all their tasks into projects, only to end up with a giant mess. They get overwhelmed, don't know where to go from there, and throw the whole system overboard. And that's a shame. Keep in mind your goal is clarity and ease. If looking at your tasks and projects makes you think, "Complicated!" then it's time to pare down your system.

Grouping tasks only makes sense if it genuinely helps you keep track of them. One project could consist of just three tasks, another—like fixing up the house—might easily include dozens.

At the moment I have nineteen active projects, both work-related and personal, though I could easily come up with more to-dos consisting of multiple tasks. But I like that my whole project list fits neatly onto one screen, so I can see everything that matters most right now. After all, the whole point of using projects is to stay on top of your main goals.

Grouping tasks into projects also prevents tasks from getting lost in the shuffle, which might otherwise happen in a situation like the one on the next page. This screenshot shows a project I'm working on that I've called *Marketing campaign*. I've got two actions due. Both are crystal clear to me, so I know exactly what I need to do. It also helps that they're grouped in a project, so I keep sight of the bigger picture. As soon as I wrap up these two actions, I'll have to come up with the next step (assuming I haven't done so along the way). If for any reason I fail to add a next step, my project will still be there in my software as a visible reminder. On the other hand, if I hadn't bothered to group these two actions into a project and had completed both without creating a next step, I might lose sight of the marketing campaign after that. I wouldn't remember it until someone asked me about it or Campbell got back to me about agencies.

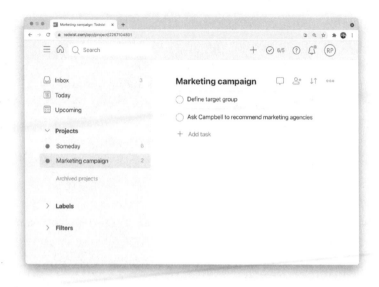

Level 5. Put labels on actions

You've moved all the open loops from your head to a to-do list in your backup brain. You've turned all your tasks into actions. And you've created projects to keep sight of the big picture. But your to-do list can do even more for you. How? With smart labels. Tagging actions with one or more labels organizes your work in ways that lets you get started faster. These are the three labels I like best:

1. ENERGY

In the last chapter, I talked about how our energy level changes over the course of the day. The more attuned we are to our own rhythms, the more we can get out of each day. Take Beethoven. It's said he ground exactly sixty beans for his first cup of coffee every morning, composed from 6:30 a.m. to 2:30

p.m., had a meal (with a nice glass of wine), and then went for a long walk. After that he parked himself in a café where he could read the paper and have a bite to eat. Or take Winston Churchill, who spent mornings in bed dictating books and letters to his secretary. He bathed twice a day and napped for an hour and a half each afternoon. This unusual routine worked well for the British statesman, who besides serving two terms as prime minister also wrote more than forty books (and won the Nobel Prize for Literature).

A workday this low key may be unusual, but I bet you have more flexibility than you think. This is where your to-do list comes in handy. Imagine you had a day of back-to-back meetings. The last one ended at 4:00 p.m., leaving you two hours to fill. It's unlikely you'll write an ultracreative proposal by 6:00 p.m. But if you've tagged your to-dos you can still make the most of that time. With a *Quick tasks* or *Low energy* label, you can group together items requiring minimal effort. Or if you're having trouble getting anywhere on a high-energy task, filter for low-effort ones you can more easily do. This works both ways. Tagging items *Deep work* or *Brainwork* can help you group focused tasks too. So you can tackle them when the time is right.

All **Low energy**

☐ Reply to Michelle's email (Low energy)
☐ Cancel double appt. for tomorrow (Low energy)
☐ Scan receipts (Low energy)

---

2. LOCATION

Labels can also be used to assign locations to tasks. That's convenient because you can take care of tasks linked to the same location in one go. Let's say you work in several different places. Maybe there are some things you can only do on-site. If there's a task you can only do at home, label it *Home*. And a label like *Office* is great to hone your focus because it gets rid of everything you can't do during office hours.

Another way to label tasks is based on specific tools or resources you need. It could be as simple as having a *printer* on hand or a *drill*. Not all the *Low energy* tasks are linked to the same location. Filtering by *Office* shows me I can start by scanning my receipts.

All	Home	Office	**Low energy**

☐ Water plants (Home) (Low energy)
☐ Reply to Michelle's email (Low energy)
☐ Cancel double appt. for tomorrow (Low energy)
☐ Scan receipts (Office) (Low energy)

3. PEOPLE

More and more work goes by email and chat these days, but for me, talking face to face still tends to get the job done better and faster. Whenever I can, I plan one-on-one meetings, even if it's just a video call. Labels let me link people's names to my to-dos. Like with my old boss Alexander. Since we both had jam-packed days, anytime our paths crossed I wanted to be absolutely sure I brought up everything on my list. Just one tap let me filter for items I needed his input on.

Labels let me add a useful extra layer to my to-do list and maximize my already fragmented time. I've noticed that some labels work better for me than others, and you'll have your own preferences. People labels may be more useful to you than labels for high- or low-energy tasks. It's just a matter of trying things out to see what works best for you.

Level 6. Outline work areas

There's one last step you can take to keep track of tasks. That's to group projects. In Level 4, I showed you how to pare a long list of to-dos into a manageable set of projects. In this next step you take those projects and group them into work areas. Like with projects, this helps you zoom out to see the big picture and filter your work even more quickly.

The first quick line you can draw is between *Work* and *Personal.* This is a really useful distinction, but why stop here? You could also try grouping projects by responsibility. Let's take my old job at Blendle as an example. As Head of Product, I was in charge of four areas:

- *Product development:* I worked to grow our user base by improving our product and adding smart features.
- *Team development:* I made sure we had the right people in the right positions, by training existing employees and hiring new ones.

- *Strategic development:* I worked on developing a vision for the company's future.
- *Self-development:* I took steps to keep growing in my job and to challenge myself.

All of my job duties normally fell into one of these four areas of responsibility. I created tags for these work areas in my to-do list, labeling them *Product, Team, Strategy,* and *Self.* Here's what that looked like in Things. This breakdown helped me keep sight of the big picture while at the same time—and maybe even more importantly—highlighting areas that were *missing* projects and activities. If *Blendle—Self* was empty, it spurred me to find a new course or fresh challenge to take on.

We all have different work areas. If *Sales growth* is part of your job, then you might group a *Marketing campaign* with that. The screenshot on the next page shows what this might look like in your task software:

You can do the same with personal projects. Group your projects related to hobbies, for example, or chores around the house. But remember to keep it simple. Add another layer of organization *only* if it helps.

RECURRING TASKS AND PROJECTS

Another useful option I love is to create recurring items. The tools I'm recommending all allow you to set recurring due dates, to stay on top of things you want to do daily, weekly, or even just once a year. It's also ideal for actions you want to integrate in your work routine. My recurring tasks have included things like reading at least one page of a book daily, reviewing the issues reported by users once a week, and drawing up a shareholder report every month.

The screenshot on the next page is a recurring task reminding me to take out the recycling every week. Here are some other good candidates for recurring to-dos:

- Going over key figures or reports
- Meeting with a coworker

- Planning vacations well ahead of time
- Checking insurance policies to update them or change providers
- Reinforcing new habits
- Routine maintenance around the house

Why not skip the list and just add these tasks straight to my calendar? Good question! Your calendar is for things you need to do on a very *specific* date. Recurring tasks, on the other hand, are things you don't want to forget but that usually aren't tied to a specific date. If I want to make sure I get a given task done on a certain day, then I will set aside that time in my calendar.

TWO-MINUTE RULE

Fantastic as it feels to have an organized to-do list with different projects and work areas, don't let that be an end in itself. To keep my own list from getting too long, I stick to the two-minute rule, another gem from David Allen: If I can do a task in under two minutes, I take care of it on the spot. One less thing to keep track of!

THE WAITING LIST

Chances are you work with other people at least some of the time and have to wait for follow-up from them occasionally. We all forget things or miss deadlines now and then. But when you need their results for work of your own, it helps to have a reliable overview of what you agreed to with whom. Here's where a *Waiting list* comes in handy. A waiting list is really just another project, like your *Someday* list. Add or move to this list everything you're waiting on others to do. That way you can see at a glance when you need to check back with them. If you'd rather not bother with a separate list, you can also use the labels I talked about earlier for this. Whatever works best for you.

USING YOUR TO-DO LIST

Let's go back to our three-stage rocket (on p. 38). Stage 1 is your calendar. Stage 2 is your to-do list. You only tackle your to-do list when you've got a gap in your calendar. In other words, anytime you don't have something scheduled to work on, you want to *automatically* reach for your to-do list. This allows your brain to really let go of the open loops and to start trusting your system, because you'll see your to-dos several times a day.

But what does this look like in practical terms? Here's the approach that works for me:

- No tasks planned for the moment? Grab your *Today* list or filter your actions by today's date. Because you've already set ballpark due dates for actions, this instantly shows you what you wanted to do today.

- Scan the list and pick what you want to work on. Can't decide? Use the Eisenhower Matrix (on p. 17) to prioritize items that are both *important* and *non-urgent.*
- Try to make a habit of getting the day's most aggravating or annoying task out of the way first.

If you have a spare moment between appointments, after lunch, or at the end of the day, take a minute to check your task inbox and rank tasks on importance. Try to check your to-do list at least once a day if you can. But don't worry if it gets away from you, because in chapter 4 I'll show you how to keep from

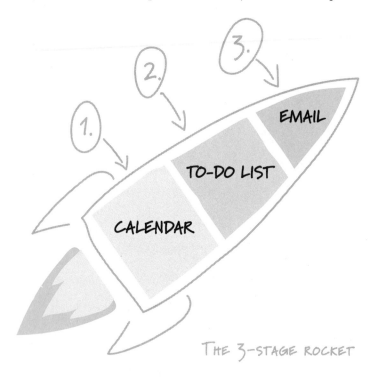

THE 3-STAGE ROCKET

missing anything, when it comes to both your calendar and your to-do list.

So now that you've built yourself a smart to-do list and a calendar you can rely on, all that's left is to actually do the work.

SEVEN MOTIVATORS

Doing the work sounds easy enough on paper, but real life tends to be different. If you're anything like me, knowing what you need to do won't always cut it. Sometimes you need a little push.

Over the years I've collected seven *motivators* that I now use daily to give myself that extra nudge. It's like I've got a toolbox I can rummage around in anytime I need to.

When you don't feel inspired to tackle a task, the motivators in the left-hand column are ideal. But if starting up is hard, so is sustaining enthusiasm for a task and bringing it to completion. That's where the motivators in the middle and right-hand columns help. Here's how.

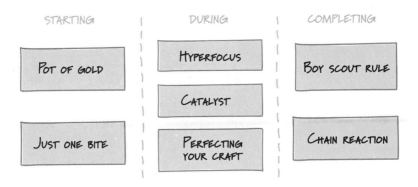

Motivator 1. Pot of gold

It's much easier to begin a task and see it through when you have a goal in mind. Especially if the job is something you're dreading or have to start up again after an interruption. A sense of purpose is a great motivator. Take a friend of mine who wants to be a doctor. He has to make sacrifices and invest tremendous energy to complete his degree. At the same time, I often hear him talk about what keeps him motivated: he wants to acquire the expertise he needs to help people. That goal is his pot of gold. Anytime he feels his motivation flagging, reminding himself of his goal fills him with fresh energy.

The *pot of gold* motivator keeps you focused and working toward your goal, even in small ways. For me, getting my morning off to a smooth start keeps me going strong throughout the workday. That motivates me to clean up the kitchen and pick up things around the house every night before I go to bed. It's not a chore I enjoy, but I know why I'm doing it.

Another example: hiring new people for my team seldom feels like my top priority because there's always all kinds of other work vying for my attention. At the same time, I know that strengthening the team will solve problems in the long run. If I keep this end goal in mind, it helps me get on top of recruitment.

Motivator 2. Just one bite

Kids are notoriously picky eaters. And who can blame them, with all those unfamiliar flavors and textures? Some parents tackle this with the *just one bite* method. The thinking is that after trying a food a few times the child will realize it actually tastes okay. It could even be the beginning of a lifelong love of—why not?—broccoli.

The one-bite motivator isn't reserved for picky eaters; it can help all of us overcome that first hurdle. Here are a few ways to use this motivator:

- *Set yourself a clear and easily achievable goal.* As soon as you reach it, you can quit. Maybe you want to write a hundred words or read five pages in that book you haven't managed to start yet. Make the task as small as you want. Writing one sentence. Reading two pages. Upon reaching your goal, you might just find you want to keep going.
- *Set limits.* Work on that proposal for ten minutes and then, if you're still stuck, stop. Those first few minutes are often enough to get into the flow of what you're doing. Alternatively, try using Francesco Cirillo's *Pomodoro Technique.* Set a timer for twenty-five minutes. Focus on your work until it goes off. Break for five minutes. Repeat.
- *Start with something fun.* For me that's picking up the Apple Pencil I got for my iPad. It's still new enough that it feels like magic. And I know that trying to draw what's in my head often brings new insight. So, if there's a task I don't feel like starting, I just grab my iPad to visualize my thoughts. See if something like this works for you too. Are there things that would get you excited about starting your work?

Motivator 3. Hyperfocus

Nothing beats that state of total focus: the feeling of complete absorption when you forget the world around you. But how long do you think we humans can actually concentrate on a single task? According to a study done at the University of California in 2005, a whopping eleven minutes—tops.[1] Other studies say we can't stick with a task for more than three minutes at a time because there's always someone who interrupts us or incoming messages that distract us. Getting back on track after a disruption can take a ton of energy. It's exhausting—and likely all too familiar.

Your workspace and setting also have a big impact on your focus. If hyperfocus always seems just out of reach or demands too much discipline, a few small workplace tweaks could make a difference. Here are some tips:

- *Switch off notifications.* Those never-ending incoming messages are killers for focus. A buzzing phone is almost impossible to ignore, and so are numbers or alerts lighting up your screen. If you want to boost concentration and focus, try switching off notifications on all your devices. After all, the whole point of notifications is to make you act. Vibrations, sounds, and bright colors instantly grab our attention. Switching them off lets you control when to pay attention to others who want something from you. On my Mac I've set the dock and menu bar to autohide unless my mouse is hovering over it. A quick Google search can help you do the same on other operating systems.
- *Close programs you're not using.* It's easier to work at a desk that's clear. That's why I recommend keeping your digital workspace cleaned up too. Get into the habit of having just one program open at a time (or only the ones you actively need). You'll keep distractions to a minimum.
- *Invest in good headphones.* I loved these for the office, but they're great for working from home too. Try noise-canceling headphones, which block ambient sound so you barely hear people around you. I'm a big fan!

- *If there's a certain kind of music that helps you work, make sure you have it on hand.* I know people who do their best work when listening to death metal. There are also services like Noisli (noisli.com) and Focus@will (focusatwill.com) that play different sounds shown to improve concentration. Or look for focus-boosting playlists on Spotify—a great one to try is *Maximum Concentration*.
- *Change up your view.* Whether you work from home or at the office, seeing people moving around out of the corner of your eye can be distracting and break your focus. Changing your literal outlook—whether this means facing a wall or being able to look out a window—is known to boost your ability to focus, if only temporarily. Experiment and figure out where you work best.
- *Work where others can see you, if possible.* I don't know about you, but I definitely get more done when I'm in an office surrounded by working people or sitting at my laptop in a café. This supervision of sorts keeps me centered on my work.
- *Find some other way to enforce concentration on yourself.* When author Rumaan Alam wanted to write a book, he used his husband's Hilton Hotel points and locked himself up in a hotel room for days at a time. It allowed him to leave behind the distraction of laundry to fold, dinners to cook, and bills to pay, and fully engage in the task of writing. Within three weeks, he had the draft for his latest novel.[2]
- *Do one thing at a time.* Whole books have been written on the concept, but it boils down to this: you'll work faster and do better work when you're not trying to complete several different tasks at once.

A remote human to help you focus

If you need some extra help to stay on task, consider using Focusmate.com. This service connects you, for fifty minutes, to a random person somewhere on the planet. You both briefly share what you'll be working on and then get to work with cameras on. If I'm stuck, this does wonders to get me back on track. You'll be amazed how well it works.

Motivator 4. Catalyst

You might remember this term from science class. In chemistry, a catalyst is a new element that's added to speed up a process. Interim results make excellent catalysts for our work. Unlike the *pot of gold* motivator, the *catalyst* is not about reaching the finish line, but about making progress.

I'm frankly surprised we don't use interim results more. When you see the work you've already done, it gives you energy that can fuel your next step. Think of it like climbing a mountain: looking back every so often to see how far you've come serves as a powerful motivator to press on. The chart on the next page shows how to make interim results work for you.

1. REACH AN INTERIM RESULT

In my experience, big projects need interim results if you're to meet the end goals. Not only will the final result be better—since integrating feedback helps you fine-tune along the way—but seeing that interim result keeps you energized and engaged.

To be useful, interim results need to check two boxes: they have to 1) be doable and 2) have value for the recipient. Say

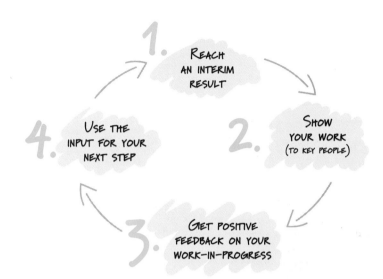

1. REACH AN INTERIM RESULT

2. SHOW YOUR WORK (TO KEY PEOPLE)

3. GET POSITIVE FEEDBACK ON YOUR WORK-IN-PROGRESS

4. USE THE INPUT FOR YOUR NEXT STEP

you're working on an important presentation. Your first interim result could be a short summary of what you aim to do in the presentation and a list of slides you'll show. The work's not done, but you have tangible progress to share.

Or let's say you land a job designing six marketing campaigns. If you work out one whole campaign for the client first, they'll have a much better picture of the final product than if you present them with storyboards for all six. In other words, your interim result already has solid value for your client.

2. SHOW YOUR WORK (TO KEY PEOPLE)

Don't assume other people will see what you're making. It's up to you to proactively share your creations as you go. I'm often struck by how little we enlist the people we know in this process. Somehow we think our work will get noticed on its own merits. If it doesn't, it must not be good enough. That's nonsense, of course.

People are busy doing their own things, so you're better off assuming your work hasn't shown up on their radar at all, instead of taking their silence as a bad sign. Be proud of what you're working on and let others know how excited you are about it!

The earlier you share your work with someone, the more it matters *who* that someone is. When you're just getting started, you want to tap positive energy. Conventional wisdom says you shouldn't expect good advice from the people you care about (your partner, parents, friends) because they're less likely to be blunt about flaws. But in the early stages, those positive responses are encouraging to hear and can keep you going.

Also, if you get stuck along the way, showing your work can help. That's because to give your client (or your reader or your user) something worthwhile, you have to clarify where you are in the process. It can be as simple as taking the draft of your presentation and adding empty slides labeled *part 2* and *part 3* to indicate there's more to come. Fresh inspiration will often strike as you go.

3. GET POSITIVE FEEDBACK ON YOUR WORK-IN-PROGRESS

Now comes the part I like best. After sharing your work with key people, you can lean back and take in their reactions. And don't be shy: this is the moment to take pride in your work. You've created something you're excited about, so shout it from the rooftops! The more energy you can derive from this stage, the more rewarding it will be.

4. USE THE INPUT FOR YOUR NEXT STEP

Besides positive responses, you may also get pointers on how your work could be improved. Those can sting, but don't just shrug them off. Put them toward your next step. If you're actively looking for more than encouragement, swap the "What do you think?" question for "Could you point me to one thing that can be improved?" Take everything into consideration, move swiftly toward your next iteration, and repeat.

Most software engineers are used to this principle. All their code is visible to colleagues, resulting in early feedback and excitement. By applying these steps, everyone can benefit from this powerful motivator.

Motivator 5. Perfecting your craft

A few years ago I watched a gorgeous documentary called *Jiro Dreams of Sushi*. It follows Jiro Ono, an aging Japanese chef (then eighty-five) in his precise and deliberate daily routine. He leaves home at the same time each day, waits to board the same train, and every day he and his team make a product celebrated around the globe. Jiro's apprentices train for months to master just one of his myriad techniques. That training isn't easy, but they take real pleasure in the work. Whether massaging an octopus for fifty minutes to get the ideal texture or cooling rice to exactly the right temperature, every detail has to be perfect. That pursuit of perfection is the point. And the movie captures it beautifully.

With this motivator, the issue isn't how to get started, but how to stay the course. That's challenging any time you're working on a big job or an ongoing one that never actually finishes. While interim results are great propellers, we can borrow a different kind of motivation from Jiro and the Japanese notion of *kaizen* that he embodies.

Kaizen is a Japanese word meaning "change for the better" or "improvement." In our busy, goal-oriented lives, we tend to value results above anything else. *Kaizen* is the opposite of that. It centers on the journey. It's about a deep appreciation for the act of work itself and continually perfecting it. This idea can be a powerful motivator to keep pushing ahead. Attention and repetition open your eyes to the beauty of your craft. You see how actions can be refined. And through this iterative cycle your actions gain a degree of predictability. That predictability has the added advantage that when you know exactly what you're doing and what your next step will be, it saves you the stress of having to choose between activities. I've become a big fan of this motivator and urge you to embrace it in your work too.

Motivator 6. Boy Scout Rule

The Boy Scout Rule is for those times when you don't feel inspired to tie up loose ends. It's something I learned from other software engineers, and it pushes you to go the extra mile.

While a programmer's job is to build new functionalities, most of their time goes to modifying snippets of existing code and fixing bugs. Once the problems have been cleared up, the original code may still be a little messy. A programmer could just leave the imperfect code as is. After all, that old code isn't part of their current task. But that's not what good programmers do. Good programmers stick to the *Boy Scout Rule*: always leave code cleaner than you found it. Just like real scouts in the wilderness.

The Boy Scout Rule is its own reward. Want to complete a task well? Do just that. Whatever you're working on, you'll always run into things that need to be straightened out or squared away. Don't let yourself be blinded by your master plan, but clean up as you go. If you notice an unpaid bill, make a note for someone to get on it. If you edit a shared document and come across older drafts, archive them. Do the job thoroughly and you'll do it better. And finishing up will be more gratifying.

Motivator 7. Chain reaction

Here's another motivator for when you're dragging your feet to the finish line. Try picturing the chain reaction your work will set off. Rarely is the job or task you're doing the actual endpoint. Usually, other people are waiting in the wings to build on your work. Your contribution, however big or small, is their starting point, and the energy you invest in your work is what takes them forward.

To spark a chain reaction, it's essential you let other people know when you're finished. If people are waiting for you to deliver, do them a favor by letting them know you're on it and will share your work as soon as it's done. Not sure if they realize you're almost finished? Most of the time you're better off communicating too much than too little.

In this chapter you started building a backup brain. You got a sense of the clarity and calm it can bring and how it frees up your own brain for what it does best: thinking. Giving yourself this gift—of using your calendar for direction and a smart to-do list for a clear head—is a fantastic start. Now for another integral part of our workday: email. Studies show employees spend an average of thirteen hours a week on email alone.[3] Can we do something about that? How can we deal with nonstop communication about work? And how can you make the most of the time you spend emailing? That's what we'll cover next.

3. FWD: RE: RE: TIME FOR EMAIL

Taking charge of your mailbox

What if I told you that from now on you could no longer read or answer emails? What would you think? That it's impossible? That you might as well wave your clients goodbye and forget about attracting any new ones? That ignoring email could cost you your job? Okay, fair enough. But if it's so important, here's my question: Do you set aside time for email in your calendar every day? If email is essential to what you do (and it certainly is for me), then it deserves a solid spot in your schedule.

In chapter 1 we looked at the nuts and bolts of your calendar and how to plan out your workweek. In chapter 2 you took on your to-do list, reclaiming your brain for more important things. Now we're going to add a third element to your week by setting aside designated times for email. That's right: as of today, email is no longer something to be squeezed in whenever you have a moment to spare.

A good way to start is by scheduling three half-hour blocks a day. In those thirty-minute blocks I try to get through as many emails as possible. Any that are left over have to wait until the next block. These blocks are spread out over my day so there's one first thing in the morning, another before or after lunch, and one at day's end. But is ninety minutes *really* enough time? For most of us: Yes. Easily.

Ignoring all the other things you have scheduled for a moment, the example below shows what this looks like in your calendar:

	Mon. 11	Tues. 12	Wed. 13	Thurs. 14	Fri. 15
8:00 a.m.					
9:00 a.m.	Email 9:00 a.m.	Email 9:00 a.m.	Email 9:00 a.m.	Email 9:00 a.m.	Email 9:00 a.m.
10:00 a.m.					
11:00 a.m.					
noon					
	Email 12:30 p.m.	Email 12:30 p.m.	Email 12:30 p.m.	Email 12:30 p.m.	Email 12:30 p.m.
1:00 p.m.					
2:00 p.m.					
3:00 p.m.					
4:00 p.m.					
5:00 p.m.	Email 5:00 p.m.	Email 5:00 p.m.	Email 5:00 p.m.	Email 5:00 p.m.	Email 5:00 p.m.
6:00 p.m.					

Even if it feels over the top at first, give this strategy a try. Because it works—and here's why:

- It lets you see how much time you actually need to stay on top of your email. That's progress, because right now you probably have no idea.
- You can keep your mailbox closed the rest of the time, since you know you'll catch up during your next email block.

- You can stop worrying that emails will slip through the cracks. Why? Because you've uncoupled email from your other work. More on that in a moment.

It wouldn't be hard to fill my entire workweek with answering all the email I get, and I'm sure you could do the same if you wanted. In fact, for years I spent way too much time on email. Sure, the people I worked with loved my speedy replies to their queries, but I had trouble getting around to my most important work. Email's like an itch: scratching only makes it worse. The more messages you send, the more you receive (usually faster than you can respond). Once you have a reputation as an instant responder, people tend to catch on pretty quick—and that has consequences. When you think about it, it's crazy we spend so much time on email. It means we're spending our days responding to and taking care of *the priorities of other people.* That's something I know all too well.

When Blendle started getting big in the Netherlands, the amount of email I had to deal with exploded. Soon my mailbox was running my days. Something had to change. I noticed I got a lot more done if I just ignored email completely during the day. While some messages were important, most could wait. The result? I pushed email to the early morning hours and evenings, and then I tackled it as before. Not surprisingly, this was not a huge success. Before long, I was working from early in the morning until late at night and making myself and the people I care about miserable. I needed a better plan. But how do you pick out the truly important stuff in that endless stream of messages? And how do you get around to your most important work without putting in overtime to keep your mailbox in check?

I don't know what your inbox looks like, but I wouldn't be surprised if you've given up on ever getting a handle on the thing. Or maybe you regularly spend a whole evening or your Saturday morning clearing out your mailbox—an approach that saps your free time and only provides temporary relief.

That's why I urge you to try something completely different. My method isn't about striving for some utopian end goal where you've taken care of all your messages and emptied out your inbox. So how does it work? At the heart of my method is this: rather than squeezing email in around other work, you give it a fixed slot in your day. During this time you work through as many emails as you can, devoting more focused attention to the task than you perhaps ever have. And that has benefits.

In a moment I'll show you how to tackle individual emails more quickly using a simple checklist in your head. The first step is to deal with email in batches.

Batching

Grouping similar kinds of activities (like email) in your calendar is simple but effective. Here's why:

- With all your tools and the right software ready to go, you save time and complete tasks with ease.
- Because the work is repetitive, it's easier to get into a flow. That's impossible when shuttling between different tasks like meetings, creative brainstorming, talking on the phone, and emailing.
- Multitasking is a myth. What really happens when we do several tasks at once is we rapidly switch back and forth. And because

it always takes some time to switch gears before we're fully focused on the task at hand, multitasking spreads our attention too thin. It's far more effective—and less stressful—to work on one thing at a time.

- You can work toward a clear endpoint because you've defined how many tasks or messages you want to get done in one go, or how long you're going to spend on it.

Thirty minutes doesn't sound like much, but you'll be surprised at how much of your mailbox you can take care of in that time. The secret is not to *eliminate* emails but to *work through* them. In a nutshell, that means you carefully read the email, decide on a follow-up action, and then communicate it to the sender.

How does this work in practice? Start at the top of your inbox and work your way down. For every email you receive, you can do one of five things:

1. You opt to turn down the request. So just communicate your decision and archive the email.
2. No action is required on your part. Simply archive the email.
3. An action is required that will take you two minutes or less. Take care of it on the spot.
4. An action is required that will take you more time, and there's a fixed deadline. Schedule the task in your calendar right away.
5. An action is required that will take you more time, but there's no fixed deadline. Then add the task to your to-do list.

The chart below shows what this looks like as a flowchart.

Whatever category an email falls into, make sure the sender hears back from you soon. The idea here is to reply as soon as you can, even if you can't get to their request at the moment. Just let them know you'll get to it later. You don't need to specify *when*, exactly.

Let's say a client asks you to send an estimate before the end of next week. You check your calendar and see an opening on Tuesday afternoon, so you block that time for the task. At this point you *could* tell your client you'll do it on Tuesday, but that leaves you without any room for error. That's why it's smarter to

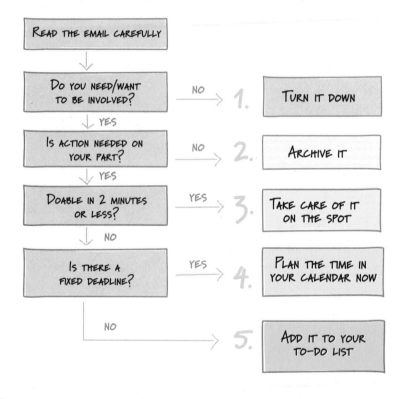

write back saying you got their request, will take a look, and get back to them next week. If you want, jot down the Friday deadline in your calendar too. That way you still have a buffer in your week.

1. Turn it down

Keep in mind that the answer to an email can always be *no*. Before accepting new work, run it through the Eisenhower Matrix from chapter 1. Does what's being asked of you fit the priorities you've set? If not, that's a good reason to turn it down.

The same goes for tasks your boss or manager asks you to do. Be selective. If you notice many of those tasks don't align with the priorities of your job, it makes sense to bring it to their attention. As convenient as it may be for you to do this one thing now, in the long run it's better for the company to be mindful about how you invest your time. The first step to that awareness is pointing out things that compromise your own work.

2. Archive it

If you've read an email and there's no action for you to take, archive it. Many people archive their emails in various folders. Maybe you do too. Now's the time to break that time-consuming habit.[1] With email search functionalities getting better all the time, retrieving messages is usually a piece of cake. (Make sure to enable email threads. That automatically brings relevant messages into view.) And because storage is also getting cheaper, the size of your mailbox likely isn't an issue either. If it is, permanently deleting a chunk of old emails from time to time is more efficient than deliberating whether to archive or delete every message that crosses your path.

My advice: simplify your life. Move emails you've dealt with into one all-purpose archive folder. If your email software doesn't have one, create a new folder and name it *Archive*. No more searching and scrolling around for the right folder each time you're done with an email. Pop it in the Archive and that's that.

3. Take care of it on the spot

Here's another great habit that can save you loads of time and trouble. If you can deal with an email in two minutes or less, just do it. Then you don't have to look for an opening in your calendar or add another item to your to-do list.

4. Plan the time in your calendar now

Emails that come with a deadline (and that will take you more than two minutes) are perfect for your calendar. That way you're sure to get the work done. Even if you know it will take less than thirty minutes, skip your to-do list and go straight to your calendar in this case.

It's also important to give yourself a buffer. Instead of scheduling work right before the due date, aim for at least a day earlier. Then if it turns out to be more work or something unexpected comes up, no sweat. And if all goes well, you can deliver ahead of schedule.

5. Add it to your to-do list

Emails that require action on your part, but don't have a fixed deadline, can go on your to-do list. Adding that new task right away will pay off later on because it saves you from having to read and understand the email all over again. And go ahead and word these tasks as actions you'll carry out (so *Call the caterer about options for lunch meetings,* not something vague like *Meeting arrangements*). When it's time to tackle the task, you'll know where to start. But don't worry yet about *when* you'll get around to the tasks here. We'll look at that in the next chapter, when we revisit your to-do list as part of planning a new week.

Once you get back to the sender about what action you'll take, you can archive the email.

Even knowing all the tricks to being ultra-efficient about email, I admit it's hard to ignore my inbox outside those scheduled times. The fact is, we're addicted to email. And that's no coincidence.

WHY IS EMAIL SO ADDICTIVE?

In his book *Hooked,* Nir Eyal breaks down how we get hooked on a product. We're all familiar with that urge to check our messages. It can be irresistible: when we wake up in the morning, while waiting in line at the checkout, even while talking to friends. According to Eyal, that's no coincidence, because email is *the* habit-forming technology. It ticks all the boxes:

1. It creates anticipation by combining the mundane and the exciting; there's no knowing which one you'll get.
2. It's extremely accessible.
3. It grabs our attention with eye-catching red dots or buzzing notifications.
4. It gives you a sense of accomplishment, which brings instant gratification.

Charles Duhigg's book *The Power of Habit* explains how this addiction works. All addictions, he says, have three things in common: a cue, a routine, and a clear reward. Our mailbox is one big jackpot of rewards (and that also goes for messaging services like WhatsApp). It delivers compliments, job offers, and messages from friends. Granted, there's also a possibility—a pretty big one, frankly—of getting bad news. But the chance we might get some great news always wins out. That's what hooks us. And even if a new email doesn't say anything earth-shattering, we still get a little reward. We feel momentarily reassured, informed, connected. A slot machine at the casino works the same way, just so you know.

Most of the time, the cue to read an email comes from our phone or computer. If you switched off these alerts after reading about hyperfocus happiness in chapter 2, you'll have cut out a big source of the problem. Aside from the constant "external trigger" of notifications, email is also an easy way out when you're feeling distracted or blocked. That's because opening and answering emails feels like getting things done (email is work, too, after all) while also offering a break from that complex and important task you're supposed to be doing.

Duhigg argues it's impossible *not* to get hooked on email. Each new incoming message feels like a little reward. But there are other ways to satisfy your brain. Keep that sense of a reward intact, and you can replace a bad habit with a healthier one. The rewards of email are different for each of us. For some, it's about connecting with people. For others, it's a mini-break from work. I know people who traded checking their email for a short walk. Another does a few push-ups whenever his focus wanders. Or you can reward yourself with a cup of coffee.

My personal fix is to stop emails from instantly showing up in my inbox so I'm not distracted by new messages whenever I open the thing. (I use Boomerang for this, a brilliant plug-in for Gmail. For more tips on apps and plug-ins to manage email, go to gripbook.com/apps.) Pick the smart tools and rewards that appeal to you, as long as they help you develop healthier email habits.

WHEN EMAIL IS POINTLESS

Not only is email addictive; often it's pointless. On their own, emails do surprisingly little for us. They're usually a surrogate for work, with the occasional nugget thrown in. It's the attachment, the presentation, or the issue at hand that's important. Just take a look at the email conversations currently in your inbox. How many are contributing directly to your top priorities? The very fact that email itself doesn't achieve much is also what makes it such a nice diversion. You can endlessly swat messages back and forth about work that needs to be done, how you plan to do it, why you should or shouldn't go down one road or another, and reiterate your viewpoint from every angle, but really you're just avoiding what you're supposed to be doing.

Escaping email

The last thing you want is to email just for the sake of it. So how can you identify an email exchange that's going off the rails? The warning signs are easy to spot. If there are more emails than people in the conversation, that's a red flag. Another is when the discussion veers far from the subject of the original email. You could do your best to steer the conversation back to the central issue, but you'll often have better luck if you switch to a different communication channel: pick up the phone, make a video call, start a chat, schedule a quick face-to-face, or drop by your co-worker's desk. While meetings are nobody's favorite pastime, putting your heads together online or in person for fifteen minutes is far more effective than another flurry of emails.

Before hitting reply, start asking yourself: *Do I really need to weigh in on this?* It sounds a tad cold, but if you don't have anything useful to add, best not to add anything at all. Of course it can help to talk this over with your team beforehand. I bet you'll soon be sending each other far fewer emails. And that helps everyone.

MORE POINTERS FOR EMAIL

Scheduling email work three times a day is a big step forward, but there are more smart tools and techniques that can help you take charge of your mailbox.

Forget about inbox zero

While it may be an effective way to keep your inbox under control, I'm not a fan of the *Inbox Zero* approach. As the name suggests, the aim is an empty inbox. Whoever reaches the bottom wins. The problem is, the focus is all wrong. Most emails you get have to do with other people's needs and priorities. You'll be happier (as will your boss) if you spend the bulk of your time on your own priorities.

Know your software

You spend loads of time using email, so it's worth exploring everything your software has to offer. There are features to personalize your reading pane, retrieve emails faster, easily email groups of people, and lots more. I tried out countless programs before choosing Gmail. The speed, powerful search functionality, and assorted other extras make it the perfect tool for me. Unfortunately, we can't always pick our software; most employers choose it for you. But don't let that stop you from finding out what your system can do.

Learn keyboard shortcuts

This goes for all software you use regularly, but for email it's a must: make time to learn keyboard shortcuts. They'll help you compose new emails, check your inbox, archive messages, and send and retrieve emails faster and easier. These are commands you perform so often that using your keyboard rather than reaching for your mouse is an instant timesaver.

Make use of templates

If you field a lot of questions by email, you might find yourself writing similar answers. You can save a ton of time by reusing your responses. Gmail has a plugin called *Canned responses* that can help. Mac and iOS have a built-in feature to help you type frequently used phrases (Settings -> Keyboard -> Text). You can go with a more sophisticated app like TextExpander, or keep it simple by using your favorite note-taking app with answers you copy-paste. This not only speeds up your process, it also helps you provide better answers—ones you can continually improve upon.

Don't rely on a system where *unread = to-do*

Lots of people get into the habit of only paying attention to messages marked unread. I don't recommend this because it's all too easy to overlook an email that you still need to deal with. If you glance at an email and forget to mark it as unread, you risk it dropping off your radar.

Try to make it as difficult as possible for you to lose track of emails. How? By always manually archiving the ones you've dealt with. That way, every message in your inbox still needs action. Can't get any clearer than that. And bonus: the final step of moving a message to your archive folder becomes super satisfying.

Guard your inbox

I always try to be critical about what enters my inbox. Newsletters and updates from sites like Facebook and Twitter create static I can do without. You can unsubscribe from many of these emails in a few clicks. If you'd rather not unsubscribe, but also don't want them littering your inbox, most email programs let you set filters to automatically archive email from certain senders.

Gmail's Priority Inbox

Use Gmail? Then here's a tool that does this job for you. Under *Inbox type* in the settings, select *Priority Inbox*. Gmail will now automatically categorize incoming emails as *Important*, *Starred*, or *Everything else*.

Settings

General Labels Inbox Accounts and Import Filters and Blocked Addresses Forwarding and POP/IMAP

Inbox type:	Priority Inbox ⌄		
Inbox sections:	1. **Starred**	Options	⌄
	2. **Important**	Options	⌄
	3. Empty	Add section	⌄
	4. **Everything else**	Options	⌄
	Reset Priority Inbox to default configuration		

This tool is not only super effective, it's also trainable, because you can click the priority marker on or off for any given email. That lets Gmail know to treat all future emails from that sender as important—or not.

ᴧ Important and unread

☐	☆	▶	Grant Schuler	Fwd: Mobile specialists available immediately — W
☐	☆	▶	Me, Rosa, Ayden	PMs — fyi, I have 3 interviews this week. 1 (Natash
☐	☆	▶	Clement la Lau	Fwd: Shareholders update: October — Hi All, You'll
☐	☆	▶	Ayden Galeh	Product Update: November — Hello everyone, hope you're
☐	☆	▶	Homerun	You have been added to the hire team for the Data

Don't check your email during meetings

One habit we all need to break right now is checking email at meetings. It's infuriating when someone you're talking to is distracted by their email while you're trying to make an important point—even if that's something most of us have been guilty of at one time or another. Worst of all is when the emailer thinks nobody else has noticed.

Emailing during meetings is a colossal waste of time and energy. Your attention's not on the task at hand, so you're wasting not only your own but also other people's time. And you're not fully focused on reading and understanding your messages either. You're lucky if your replies even make sense. If this happens to be you, take another critical look at the three blocks you scheduled for email each day. Are these the best times in your day? Is it critical that you reply during a meeting? On the flip side, if you're sitting through a stale meeting to which you have nothing to add, then *that's* what needs to be fixed.

Want to write better emails? Then take your time. My top three tips for sending effective emails are: know what you want to accomplish, keep it short, and be proactive.

Know what you want your email to accomplish

Before you start typing, it helps to stop and think about the purpose of your email. Do you want a response? Do you just want to inform? Or to activate? Are you trying to persuade the reader? If you have a clear goal, you'll compose better emails.

Keep it short

No matter what the purpose of your email, make it shorter. Get straight to the point. More often than not you want something from the recipient, but since everybody's busy, a long email screams "difficult." On the other hand, an email that's brief and to the point and asks a concise question seems "doable" and so is more likely to get a faster and better response. Got lots of questions? Consider splitting them up over a couple of emails, or else discuss them by phone or face-to-face.

Also, take a tip from marketers, who have perfected the art of giving their newsletters clickable subject lines. A clear subject immediately clues your recipient in to what you want from them. Let's say you want feedback on a short proposal. Then a good subject line is, "Could you take a look at this short proposal?"

Communicate proactively

If your goal is to spend less time on email, then a good place to start is by communicating proactively. How? Think ahead: rather than asking open-ended questions, make a suggestion. Then your recipient only needs to answer *yes* or *no*. The busier that person is, the better this works, but in the end it's nicer for everyone. To see why, take a look at this email exchange:

Me: Hi! I got your address from your colleague and would like to meet up for coffee sometime to discuss Project X.

Other: No problem, sounds great. When's good for you?

Me: Wednesdays and Thursdays work best for me—what would be a good time?

Other: I'm free on Thursday at 2:00 p.m. Where should we meet?

Me: How about at your office in Amsterdam?

I could have avoided this whole rigamarole by making a suggestion myself in my first email. If the other person is busier than you, offer three or four times and locations. By offering alternatives right off the bat, your appointment could be made with a single reply, like this:

Me: I'd like to meet for coffee sometime to discuss X. Would it be convenient for you to meet next Wednesday at your office in Amsterdam, say at 10:00 a.m.? I'm available that whole day, or any time after 11:00 a.m. on Thursday.

Other: Wednesday won't work for me, but I've got time on Thursday at 2:00 p.m. See you then!

For most of us, electronic communication isn't limited to email. Lots of companies use other messaging services, and with good reason. Coworkers might start a WhatsApp group to stay in the loop, and at Blendle we used Slack. While emailing's easy, the threshold for getting in touch using WhatsApp and Slack is even lower. And because conversation histories are saved, sharing knowledge is simple, everybody's more connected, and there's less chance of needlessly duplicating work. Communication is faster and easier since everyone's always on the chat.

Clearly there are benefits to these services, and they can help save us all valuable time. But just like with email, we have to decide how we use messaging. Because there's a big downside: with chat programs we tend to expect an immediate response. That convenience of getting quick answers comes with tremendous pressure to reply, especially when you get work-related messages after hours. Once you've seen a message—urgent or not—it's impossible to unsee it. And good luck leaving it until morning.

Want to get the most out of Messenger, WhatsApp, Slack, or Teams? Here are my tips:

- *Turn off notifications.* If you're going to focus on your most important work, you can't have these apps interrupting you all the time. Worried about missing a critical message from your boss? Most services let you add exceptions. With WhatsApp you can opt to mute new message notifications for certain groups or individuals, and Slack gives you this option too (per person or per channel). Slack has a handy *Do not disturb* status, for when you want to unplug and get some concentrated work done. I would suggest muting as much as you can get away with. You can always check in later and catch up. Just make sure everyone knows how to reach each other in case of a work emergency.

- *Use the status setting.* Slack and Teams both have a status bar that lets you say in a few words where you are or what you're doing. That lets people know if you're away on business, in a meeting, on vacation, or at your desk. No need to ask, which means less hassle for everyone.

- *Come right out with it.* One thing that bugs people about chatting is messages that begin with "Hey!" and then wait for a reply before posing the question. Though the sender is being friendly and low-key, for the recipient it's annoying because they're "forced" to reply right away, with no idea what's coming.

- *Treat chats like emails.* When people ask me something using Slack or WhatsApp, I process their message the same way I do a new email. Will it take me two minutes or less? Then I deal with it on the spot. If I need more time, I put the task on my calendar or add it to my to-do list. Integrating these instant messages into my routine this way reduces the risk of any important work slipping through the cracks.

- *Learn keyboard shortcuts.* Just like with email, shortcuts can save you lots of time on messaging apps. It pays to learn them by heart.

In this chapter you've set aside time in your workweek for email and other communication. If it feels like a lot to take in, start by scheduling those three half-hour blocks for email each day. You can go back through this chapter at your own pace and add other elements one at a time.

Email completes stage 3 of our rocket, but we're not quite done. Because now that you're building a smart system using the tools in the first three chapters, how do you keep it up?

4. WORKING WITH A NET

Experience the clarity and peace of mind a Friday recap brings

Your calendar's all set, your to-do list ready to go, and you've got fixed times to focus on email each workday. Way to go! You've laid the basis for clarity and peace of mind. But it doesn't stop there. Because without regular maintenance, the system will crumble.

Upkeep requires just one simple routine: each week, take thirty minutes of your time to update your calendar and clean up your to-do list.

I first read about doing a "weekly review" in David Allen's *Getting Things Done*, and now I can't live without it. It's a straightforward yet powerful tool, and I'll guide you through setting it up.

Why once a week, and not daily or monthly? Good question. Picture your kitchen. If you leave the dishes to pile up in the sink for a week, it soon turns into a hazard site. Striving for clean countertops and an empty dishwasher every moment of every day, on the other hand—that's never going to happen. Immediately washing each dirty dish would be hugely inefficient. But not washing them leaves you without dishes at some point. As with doing dishes, staying on top of things at work is about striking the right balance. And for work, I've found that once a week is just right. That keeps the flexibility in your workweek without losing sight of the big picture.

A weekly review—or as I call it, my *Friday recap*—is about creating a safety net under your workweek. No matter how chaotic your days get, with cascading meetings and fires to put out, a Friday recap gets you back on track. In fact it allows you to be *more* chaotic during the week, because you know you'll regroup on Friday.

A Friday *what*?

A Friday recap is a date you make with yourself once a week to a) look back on the past workweek and b) look ahead to the workweek to come. Knowing you've set aside this time to take stock and make plans each week means you don't have to worry about loose ends the rest of the time. If there's anything you don't get around to or that slipped through the cracks, you'll catch it in this session. It helps you keep on top of things, but you need only thirty minutes a week to do it. And did I mention it gives you peace of mind for the rest of the week?

Finding the best moment

I always do my weekly recap on Friday afternoons. Why Friday? Simple. I want to start the weekend with a clear head and a clean slate. It feels great to go over my calendar and to-do list on Friday afternoons. That way I know I've caught and rescheduled everything I didn't get to in the past week, and I've set priorities and made a plan for the week ahead. That makes it easier to leave work behind for the weekend. But I also know people who prefer to do their recap on Saturday or Sunday. Another friend opts for Monday morning because that gives him fresh energy for the week. Whatever you choose, the important thing is to pick a day and time you can stick to.

How long does a weekly recap take? Normally, thirty minutes is plenty of time. But to start, give yourself about ninety minutes to organize everything you'll need.

When I explain the thinking behind the Friday recap, most people are instantly on board. Clarity and peace of mind about my workweek? Who would say no to that? But I've also seen people struggle with getting started. So let's get that out of the way first. Stop reading for a moment and set aside ninety minutes in your calendar, at whatever time you want. (As I said, after the first session it goes much faster.) Don't worry, it's not complicated. If you can commit to doing a recap four times, you'll have gotten the hang of it. But it's the most powerful tool around for taking your work to a higher level.

Next question: How do you do a Friday recap? Well, there are two parts: You look back on your week. Then you look ahead at the week to come.

PART 1. LOOKING BACK

Your Friday recap starts with surveying the damage of the past week and cleaning up. Don't worry if you suddenly see just how much got lost in the shuffle. That's the whole point of this session—so you can do something about it. Here we go.

1. Check your calendar

This is the part that gives me the most peace of mind the rest of the week. And it's incredibly simple. Here's how it works. I click through each meeting and work block I'd planned for the past week and ask:

- Did I take any notes? Or are there meeting minutes? (If so, I go through them and add any actions I need to take to my to-do list.) Are there any other items I want or need to follow up on?
- Is a follow-up appointment needed? If so, has it been scheduled?
- Have I done everything I planned to do this past week? Have I updated everyone I needed to check in with?

2. Run through inboxes of all kinds

You've probably added plenty of new items to your to-do list's *inbox* over the past week. This is a good time to turn all those tasks into actions (if you haven't already) so they're clear-cut and doable. When that's done, you can drag them into their respective projects, if applicable.

You may have more types of inboxes, so take a moment to check for any other loose ends. Your inboxes can include:

- A notebook
- Scribbled memos lying around your desk
- A note-taking app, like Notion or Microsoft OneNote
- Your email inbox (Just do a quick scan to make sure you haven't overlooked anything major this week. Don't get sucked into email work.)
- And don't forget about snail mail, files in your *Downloads* folder, photos you've taken, videos you've made, and conversations in chat apps. Check them all to see if you need to do any follow-up.

3. Check your ongoing projects

Go through projects in your task system one by one:

- Read through each task in the project, rewording any vague tasks into clear, doable actions. Check for open action items that need updating. And most important, make sure you've identified the next step for each project. If not, now's the time to do so.
- Are there any new projects you need to add? Or old ones you can check off your list?
- Are all your projects and designated work areas (as described in chapter 2) still current? This is key. It's the way to keep from missing anything.
- Are there people on your *Waiting for* list that should get a quick reminder?
- Don't forget to take a look at your *Someday* list. Are there tasks or projects you could start on next week?

PART 2. LOOKING AHEAD

With all the information you gathered in part 1 of your Friday recap, you now have a clear sense of what's important for the near future. Keep that in mind. Next up: building your next week.

Plan your calendar for next week

I walked you through how to plan a workweek in detail in chapter 1. We're going to do that again now. Here's a quick refresher:

- Choose work that's aligned with your responsibilities and goals.

- Balance urgent and important work. Try to set aside as much time as you can for *important* and *non-urgent* tasks.
- Less is more. Plan conservatively, because we tend to pile too much on our plates. Try to pare down your priorities for this week to only two or three things.

With these priorities in mind, you can plan out your week. Here are the six steps I run through:

1. Block time for all your priority work, meetings, and appointments.
2. Have all meetings been confirmed by the people attending?
3. Have you included travel time for meetings elsewhere?
4. Have you scheduled the prep time you'll need for meetings?
5. Is there any information you still need for a given meeting?
6. It's likely you already had some things on your schedule this week. Are any now unnecessary or redundant? And can you cancel?

Goals

At this point, you may not have set any concrete goals. That's to be expected, as most of our plans and dreams exist only half-formed in our heads. In chapters 5 and 6 I'll help you set out your goals. Once you've formulated them for yourself, your weekly recap will be the perfect time to run through your goals one by one and make sure you've outlined the next step for each.

At Blendle we did team-based evaluations four times a year to take stock of the past quarter. One issue that came up like clock-work was that when scheduling work, we all tended to overlook our own goals. What a missed opportunity! That taught me to make my goals the basis for each new week.

Personal checklist

The next step is to create a basic checklist for your Friday recap. Include items that are important to you, your work, and your personal life. For years my checklist included "Review notes from the Product Team meeting." I made that a recurring action because I wanted to take an extra good look at those notes each week. I know someone who has "Create backup" as a fixed item on his checklist, and an HR manager whose list includes "Send out email with staff news." In other words, it's up to you to decide the focus of your weekly recap. A personalized list lets you make the most of this system. Here's what my own checklist looks like:

FRIDAY RECAP CHECKLIST	
STANDARD CHECKLIST	**RICK'S LIST**
LOOK BACK	
Review calendar + meeting notes	Review calendar + meeting notes
Run through inboxes	Run through inboxes
Review projects	Review notes from the Product Team meeting
	Review projects
	Clear desktop and downloads
	Rate my energy level + note any insights

FRIDAY RECAP CHECKLIST	
STANDARD CHECKLIST	**RICK'S LIST**
LOOK AHEAD	
Fill in calendar	Fill in calendar
	Review goals
	Pay all open invoices
	Reread personal mission (more on this in chapter 5)

Take it to the next level: reflecting on your week

The Friday recap is a perfect time to clean up your to-do list and plan your next workweek. It's also a great opportunity to reflect on your week and gain some valuable insight into what works and what doesn't. One thing I do is rate my energy level on a scale of 1 to 10 and jot down why. That helps me detect patterns in my workflow. Here are other questions you could consider adding to your recap:

- What accomplishment or personal triumph are you most proud of this week?
- Did you accomplish your top priorities, as planned? Why or why not?
- What was the biggest lesson you learned this week? What's the takeaway for next week?

Help!

I've been training people to do weekly recaps for quite a while now. Everyone—without exception—says this simple system enables them to tie up loose ends and start each new week with a better plan. Still, there are some pitfalls to watch out for. The most common problem I hear is, "I schedule my recap every Friday but then I don't do it." Does this sound familiar? You know the peace of mind a recap brings, but can't seem to make it happen? Here are some things that can help:

- How well do you stick to what's in your calendar? Remember: Your calendar is sacred. It's the rock you build your week on. That may take a little getting used to, but the better you stick with your plan for the week, the better it will work for you. Your Friday recap is part of that plan.
- Is anxiety holding you back? Feeling overwhelmed at the thought of all those loose ends and stray to-dos? That's only natural. But don't let it discourage you. Just try again. Ignoring or avoiding work won't make it go away. Plus, putting the Friday recap in your calendar means it has not only a fixed start time but a fixed stop time too. When you reach the end of that time block, just stop. Then schedule part 2 and finish up another time.
- Is the timing right? As I said, I like to do my weekly recap on Friday afternoons. That way I have a distinct finish line at the end of my week and a clear view of the next. It's a great way to head into the weekend. But play around with the timing to find the moment that's right for you. If you're often called to put out fires on Friday afternoon, Friday morning might work better, before things get hectic. Or you could try a quiet moment on the weekend. Or turn it into a treat. A friend of mine does his weekly recap as an extended coffee break, with a cappuccino as his reward.

- Is your personal checklist too long? Or too vague? If your re-cap keeps snagging at the same point, there's a risk you'll start skipping the rest. That's a sign you need to simplify your list.
- Do you have a hard time sticking to a schedule? Try buddying up with someone and doing your weekly recap together. It doesn't have to be your closest coworker, just anyone who gives you that extra nudge you need. In chapter 7 we'll look at how to recruit this ally.
- Is your Friday recap taking too long? If you're finding it hard to finish, you may be biting off more than you can chew. For now, just concentrate on getting things clear and up to date. No crossing off tasks as you go! I know it's tempting to get some actual work done during the organizing process, but if you're in a perpetual time crunch it's better to save the work itself for later. First, focus on the recap.
- After the first few times, your Friday recap will start to come naturally. At that point you can try throwing in the two-minute rule: if you come across a task you can complete in two minutes or less, do it then and there. Save everything else for your to-do list or calendar.

I've created a crash course to help you out. Sign up at grip-book.com/fridayrecap, and I'll send you inspiration each week to help you get this powerful tool under your belt.

If you do just one thing to improve your workweek, make it the Friday recap!

CHEAT SHEET
FOR PART 1

Working with a calendar (p. 5)

- Put all your meetings and appointments in your calendar.
- Specify clear start and stop times.
- Send out invites.
- Include travel, prep, and admin time.
- And most important: schedule your own work on priority projects.

Figuring out your priorities (p. 13)

- Make an overview of your responsibilities (refer to your job description and company objectives).
- Based on those responsibilities, draw up a list of main work tasks and pass on as many *urgent* and *not important* tasks as you can.
- Create focus by narrowing down this work list to two or three priorities.
- For each priority, come up with the first step you can take.
- Set aside time in your calendar next week for each step.

Checking your plan for the week (p. 19)

- Have you set aside enough prep time for meetings?
- Have you invited everyone you want to attend?
- Is the location or meeting link all set?

- Does your calendar reflect your priorities?
- Have you set aside time for email?
- Are you getting the most out of your working hours? Have you scheduled creative work and more routine tasks at optimal times? Does your schedule limit the need to switch between meetings and creative work?
- Have you scheduled your most important work early in the week?
- Have you left yourself enough of a buffer?

Dealing with unexpected work (p. 29)

- Does the task really need to be done this minute?
- Make a generous estimate of how long it will take.
- Schedule the task in your calendar.
- Check for conflicting appointments and let those people know you'll need to reschedule.
- Add any follow-up tasks (like rescheduling appointments) to your to-do list.

Working with a to-do list (p. 39)

- Pick your software (see gripbook.com/apps).
- Add all your tasks to your digital to-do list.
- Word your tasks as doable actions.
- Group your actions into projects.
- Add labels to quickly filter your actions.
- Outline work areas.

Making time for email (p. 77)

- Schedule three thirty-minute blocks a day for email.
- Turn off email notifications.
- Unsubscribe from newsletters you don't read.

- Learn your email program's keyboard shortcuts.
- Write shorter emails.
- Communicate proactively to reduce back-and-forth (for instance, when arranging a meeting, suggest dates up front).

Sorting through your messages, one by one (p. 81)

- No action is required on your part. Simply archive the message.
- You opt to turn down the request. Let the sender know.
- You can complete the work in two minutes or less. Take care of it on the spot.
- It's going to take some time, and there's a fixed deadline. Schedule the task in your calendar.
- It's going to take some time, but there's no fixed deadline. Add the task to your to-do list.

Friday recap checklist (p. 97)

- Look back over your week.
- Review your calendar and meeting notes.
- Run through inboxes of all kinds.
- Check up on ongoing projects.
- Recap the progress you made on your goals.
- Now look ahead to the coming week.
- Plan out your workweek using your calendar, to reflect your goals and priorities.

PART 2

GRIP

AND YOUR

YEAR

magine a farmer who didn't think about when he did which jobs, and instead did whatever felt right at the time. He almost certainly wouldn't go out in the cold season to prepare the fields for harvest at the far end of summer. Or what if the average marathon runner didn't devise a training plan? She might never get out of bed and brave the elements at the crack of dawn for a race still months away.

You can't feel your way to a harvest or a marathon. You have to commit to a plan.

And that commitment starts early. Because first you need to know *what* you want to grow. Or *why* you want to run. Some people have clear-cut goals and five-year plans, but what about those of us who don't?

In part 1 of this book we zoomed in on the *hows* of our work. Now we're going to switch gears and focus on the *whats* and the *whys*. What drives you? And why? Many of us don't take the time to ponder these questions all that deeply. Maybe we're wary of the ramifications they could have for our already busy lives. Or maybe we do have goals in mind but never really take the time to spell them out.

In the next three chapters I'll show you how to figure out what you really want. I'll walk you through how to create a plan with goals for the year. And how you can make those goals actually happen, one step at a time. Finally, we'll look at one of my favorite techniques for seeing things through: a weekly session with a *partner in crime*.

5. WHAT GETS YOU OUT OF BED?

Discovering what drives you

What do I really want? It's an incredibly important question, but one many people are afraid to ask. Don't be! You miss out on so much when you avoid it.

In the first chapters we focused on making things happen—on how to harness your calendar and to-do list to get more of your priority work done. In this chapter we're going to turn from daily practice to the more fundamental matter of what motivates you and why.

Over the next pages I'll be throwing all kinds of questions your way. To get the most out of this chapter, I recommend jotting down your answers as you go.

The quest to figure out what drives you can be as complicated as you want to make it. My approach is simple: *doing things* is the best way to find out what you enjoy doing. Try things out, keep what you like, lose the rest. Nothing's set in stone.

I believe in setting goals to move my work forward. And of course I'm not alone. Countless studies show that having something to work toward makes a difference.[1] But to set goals, you first need to look at that fundamental question of what makes you excited. In my own search I learned there are three pieces to this personal puzzle: your passions, your skills, and your mission.

Your passion

In 2005, Apple founder Steve Jobs gave a stirring speech at Stanford University about following your passion.[2] He told students: "You've got to find what you love. . . . The only way to do great work is to love what you do. If you haven't found it yet, keep looking. Don't settle. As with all matters of the heart, you'll know when you find it." According to Jobs, you shouldn't feel restricted when thinking about your passion but let your imagination run wild. Ask questions like:

- What activities can make you lose track of time?
- What can you always read, hear, or watch more of without ever getting bored? What can't you get enough of? What fascinates you?
- What do you know more about than most people?
- If time or money (or other constraints) were no object, what would you most like to spend a few months doing?

But of course passion isn't the only thing that drives you. There are two more pieces to this puzzle: your skills and your mission.

Your skills

In his book *So Good They Can't Ignore You*, Cal Newport talks about what he calls the *craftsman mindset*. Whereas passion centers on the question *What can the world offer me?* the craftsman mindset centers on *What can I offer the world?* According to Newport, the craftsman mindset is a more fruitful place to start your search. Start out by doing something you're good at and follow that path until you find your passion. Starting out from your passion is risky, he says, because there's always only a small overlap between what you want and what the world wants. It's not easy to make your passion pay.

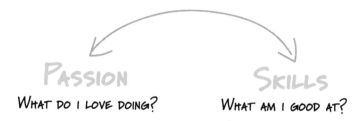

When hiring people, I'm always looking for a craftsman mindset: people who are good at what they do *and* passionate about it.

So what are *your* skills? These questions can yield some clues:

- What are you good at? What things come naturally to you that benefit those around you—things you might not immediately think of or notice?
- Ask yourself, *What can I offer the world?* What comes to mind?

So, besides following your passion, it's every bit as important to follow what you're good at. This brings us to the third puzzle piece.

Your mission

So far, so good. But there's another layer to what drives you. Even Steve Jobs didn't go to work every day just because he loved it. He wanted to accomplish something. Back when he founded Apple, he defined that something like this: "To make a contribution to the world by making tools for the mind that advance humankind." In other words, he had a mission.

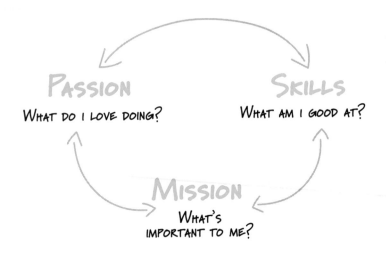

Stephen Covey turned this idea into one of his famous "7 habits of highly effective people": *Begin with an end in mind.* He suggests imagining you've just died. Then write down what your family and friends would say about you at your memorial service. How do you want to be remembered after you're gone? If this exercise doesn't do it for you, no problem. There are more ways to think about what's important to you.

Fadumo Dayib is a woman with a mission. She was born in Kenya to Somali parents who'd fled their own country after losing eleven children to treatable diseases. When the family was deported from Kenya back to Somalia, she soon had to flee herself. This time from civil war. Dayib and her younger siblings made it to Finland, where they were granted asylum. She'd learned to read at the age of fourteen, went to nursing school in Finland, earned two master's degrees and is working on her PhD. In 2014, she declared her ambition to move back to her home country to run for president, in the first Somalian elections since 1984. On her website she writes: "My goal is to help rebuild post-conflict Somalia through informed political leadership," and says her "calling in life, other than being a dedicated mother to my four children, is the development of Somalia. It is to serve humanity." That's about as big and as clear as a mission can get.

Finding your mission is a very personal journey. I hope Dayib's story helps you make your mission a bold one and let nothing stand in your way. Does it have to be presidential or heroic? Not at all. But it's good to realize it *can* be.

Whatever you think about Elon Musk and that plan to put people on Mars, his thoughts on *impact* can be useful here. He measures impact by multiplying the amount of good something does by the number of people affected. That means a small amount of good for a large group has as much impact as a large amount of good for a handful of people. Here are some other prompts to help you discover your own mission:

- Do Stephen Covey's exercise: How would you like to be remembered?
- How could you do a small amount of good for the largest number of people? Which passions and skills could you enlist for this?
- What makes you angry? This strong emotion can be a hint to where your mission lies.

These three puzzle pieces—passion, skills, and mission—become more meaningful once you get to work on them. Try writing down your thoughts about each one, starting on page 121. It doesn't need to be anything complicated. The way I do this is with a note in Evernote listing my three puzzle pieces in brief bullet points. This is a living memo, but at the moment it looks like this:

Mission

What's important to me?

- I want to make the world a little better every day:
  - through the work I do
  - through the projects I do outside of work
  - by doing my part to save the planet and help close the gap between rich and poor
  - by nurturing close and loving relationships with my family

Passion

What do I love doing?

- I like making things other people can use
- I enjoy solving problems
- I love finding ways to make slow things faster or complicated things easier
- I like doing things that are useful
- I love building things from scratch

Skills

What am I good at?

- I'm good at putting things in motion

- I'm good at making complicated things simple
- I'm very self-disciplined
- I'm a good listener
- I'm good at thinking strategically
- I'm good at prioritizing

I always read through this memo as part of my Friday recap (see chapter 4). It helps me keep sight of what drives me and I can check to see if my actions align with that. Whenever I learn something new about myself, I update my puzzle pieces to match.

MISSION

What's important to me?

-
-
-
-

PASSION

What do I love doing?

-
-

-
-

SKILLS
What am I good at?

-
-
-
-

Get moving

Good friends of mine sold their home some time back to travel around Europe in a camper. Herman and Sietske have been on the road for a year now and they've never been happier. The puzzle pieces of passion, skills, and mission all fell into place for them. They wanted to live free (*passion*), and because they're both musical and good with their hands (*skills*) they've been able to fix up their van themselves, while earning money along the way. It's also important to them (*mission*) to be open to the people they meet on their travels. This nomadic lifestyle turns out to be ideal for them at this stage, but it wasn't some stroke of luck. It took months of brainstorming and planning.

There's only one way to find out whether what's in your head is what you genuinely want: by trying it out. You can philosophize until you're blue in the face about whether trading your house for a camper is the right move, but the only surefire way to find out is to do it.

1. **THINK**
— ABOUT YOUR MISSION
— ABOUT YOUR PASSIONS
— ABOUT YOUR SKILLS

2. **GET STARTED**
— MAKING RESOLUTIONS
— TURNING RESOLUTIONS INTO CONCRETE THINGS TO TRY

3. **TRY THINGS OUT**
— MAKE THOSE CONCRETE THINGS HAPPEN
— SEE WHAT YOU THINK, THEN MAKE ADJUSTMENTS

Discovering what you want starts with thinking about your personal mission, passion, and skills (1). Once you've defined these three puzzle pieces, you can get moving by making a resolution for each puzzle piece (2), and then turning those resolutions into concrete things to try out (3).

Do your mission, passions, or skills suggest you should be doing a different kind of work? Or pursuing other hobbies? The more a resolution fits with your three puzzle pieces, the better it will fit you. Your resolutions don't need to be life-changing, like those of my nomadic friends. They can be modest things like volunteering at the food bank, or trying your hand at coaching Little League, or taking a public speaking course. The resulting experiences will help you figure out more precisely what you really want.

So how do you turn a puzzle piece into a resolution? Here's an example:

- Mission: It's important to me to stand up for the equal treatment of men and women
- Resolution: to join an organization that works to advance this objective, or
- Resolution: to work to change our company culture so everyone gets equal treatment, or
- Resolution: to start a book club to discuss this issue with friends

As you can see, these resolutions—all three of which stem from your mission—can vary widely in scope. Choosing one and acting on it helps you find out if this mission truly motivates you. Turning the passion and skills puzzle pieces into resolutions works the same way. If you're excited about woodworking, sign up for a class to see if it's more than just a passing fancy. Or take a cue from my father. He took up drumming at the tender age of fifty-six to see if he had a knack for it. [Narrator: *Turns out he did.*]

Want some more pointers for coming up with resolutions? This is what helps me:

- Realize that choices are very often reversible and that it's okay if you don't get it right in one go. Resolutions and what you do with them are usually easy to change or undo.
- Thanks to my Friday recap, I regularly reflect on my choices. And I've learned that resolutions that initially made me a little apprehensive were ultimately the most rewarding. So look back more often and use the insight that gives you.
- Not pursuing your mission, passions, or skills means by definition you're choosing in favor of something else. Saying *no* to that new job is also saying *yes* to your current workplace. Is that a choice you're happy with?

If you don't translate your resolutions into concrete actions, the odds you'll do anything with them are slim. Take the resolution: "To change our company culture so everyone gets equal treatment." That's a great aspiration, but hard to act on. Make it more concrete, however—"To help change our company culture by recruiting a working group to write a handbook on gender equality"—and you've turned it into an action. And resolutions in the form of action are the perfect springboard for your goals.

Many people have difficulty setting achievable goals for their work and personal lives. Before we take a closer look at how to do this, let's take a step back and ask: *Why is it a good idea to set goals in the first place?*

A goal is a milestone

I'm a big fan of setting personal goals. They help me focus on what's most important. And they help me decide what *not* to work on. I always get much more done if I have a clear outcome to work toward—and I see that with other people too. But you don't have to take my word for it.

Edwin Locke and Gary Latham have been researching the importance of setting goals since 1974. Based on their joint research, where they reviewed hundreds of studies, they developed their Goal-Setting Theory.[3] This theory describes that goals can be an effective way to increase productivity. As long as you use them correctly. The key? A clear, challenging enough *what* and a specific *when*, combined with regular feedback on how you're doing. I'll show you how to do all of that.

I know some people are allergic to the word *goal*. It feels too big and weighty, maybe because of impossible targets set by a boss or someone else. Or perhaps you got excited about a personal goal in the past that turned out to be unattainable. If you've had negative experiences like these, you may not be keen to set goals.

Even so, I'm hoping to get you excited about pursuing new goals in a new way. In my method, goals aren't a final destination but a milestone along the way, where you can stop for a moment to catch your breath and celebrate how far you've come. Reaching goals feels fantastic. And you can make them as small and doable as you want—a trick I swear by.

Goals energize you

I bet you've experienced that burst of energy when a goal comes into view—when you round the last corner in a race and see the finish line up ahead. That last stretch before you is clear and doable, and one final push is all it takes. With goals you get that same rush, that same extra boost.

SETTING GOALS

Whether you reach your goals depends chiefly on how carefully you set them. A well-formulated goal can make all the difference between getting to that finish line and giving up halfway. You've likely heard of the SMART approach to setting goals. This is the rule that goals should be Specific, Measurable, Achievable, Realistic, and Timely. While there's nothing wrong with those criteria, I prefer something a little less complicated. That's why I test my goals on only two indicators.

1. Am I excited about it?

If you base your goals on your passion, skills, and mission, then they can't help but get you excited. That's why I've made this the main criterion for my own goals. The idea of going for a goal has to fire my enthusiasm, and reaching it should be something to celebrate. Standard criteria like *achievable, realistic,* or *measurable* fall flat in comparison.

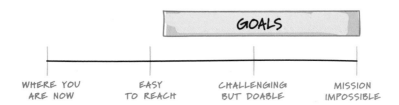

Your enthusiasm for a goal hinges in part on how much of a challenge it presents. How much effort will it take to achieve? There's no point setting goals you can't reach, but they shouldn't be *too* easy either. One of the keys to staying motivated is to set goals that fall between these two extremes.

But what about goals set for you by your boss or manager? What can help is trying to understand their enthusiasm. Why does this goal matter to your boss? (Sometimes you'll discover that you don't share your boss's values. If that happens a lot, it might be time to ask if you're in the right job.) Hearing why my boss is so psyched often makes a big difference. And once you get a glimpse into *why* a goal matters, that can give you the motivation you need to meet it.

2. Will I know when I get there?

Knowing beforehand when you've actually reached your goal is incredibly important. Countless studies show this, and I've seen it personally time and again: if your goals aren't specific, you'll have trouble reaching them. At Blendle, one of my responsibilities was to think about company strategy. No one needed to convince me this was important, so enthusiasm wasn't an issue. In terms of making this a goal for myself, I could have called it something like *Think about Blendle's future*. But then how would I know when I was done? If instead I said my goal was to *Present plans for the rest of the year by June 1*, then there's no doubt where the finish line is. So when formulating a goal it's vital you have a clear answer to the questions *When are we there? When is it done?* A good way to test if the outcome is clear enough is to ask: *Will other people be able to tell when I've reached my goal?*

If the answer is yes, it's specific enough.

In practical terms, goals requiring you to plan ahead more than three months are tricky. The finish line is just too far away. I try to keep goal deadlines within the next quarter. With larger projects, you'll want to split up the goal into smaller chunks.

Stretch goals

President John F. Kennedy wanted to put the first man on the moon. Fadumo Dayib set her sights on the highest office in Somalia, which has never been held by a woman. Jody Williams wants to rid the planet of land mines. And Bill Gates wants to eradicate malaria. These are gutsy goals, sometimes called BHAGs—Big Hairy Audacious Goals. I prefer the term *stretch goals*. If you're not feeling challenged by the goals you have now, then it's time to add some stretch.

Setting a good stretch goal is an art in itself. The goal lies beyond your normal reach, but not far enough that you'll never get there. If you want to motivate and challenge yourself to strive for a big goal, it has to fall somewhere between *impossible* and *tough but doable.* When JFK announced on May 25, 1961, that he planned to send a man to the moon that decade, it was a clear if seemingly out-of-reach target. At the same time, everyone on Earth could *picture* a rocket ship going to the moon. And that's a second element of a stretch goal.

If you want set yourself a good stretch goal, see how it rates on this checklist:

- I can clearly picture achieving this goal.
- Thinking about this goal makes me a little apprehensive.
- I have no idea how I'll ever be able to achieve this goal.
- People around me openly question whether I can do it.
- The idea of achieving this goal makes me super excited.

Both goals and stretch goals help move you forward. In my experience, having a mix of both kinds of goals works best. I might have one or two really big, ambitious goals, plus a handful of smaller, doable goals that I'm sure to reach with some time and effort.

Because you want to give yourself the best odds of reaching your goals, be careful not to set too many at once. I don't recommend more than seven, tops. Remember: less is more. That said, I always like to have at least four goals in the pipeline. If I get stuck on one, then I can always shift focus to another.

Documenting goals

Now for practical matters: How do you keep track of goals? As with your calendar, to-do list, and email, there's a world of tools to choose from. But I like to write down my goals in a blank Google Docs file.

You can see that I've set myself six goals for the end of June, and I've already reached two of them. They all have the same deadline. I like using Google Docs for this because it offers me a simple blank page where I'm free to jot things down however I want. And this program makes it easy to share any or all of my goals with others.

Of course, lots of companies have their own systems where employees can document goals they set with their managers. I got into the habit of adding work goals to my Google Docs list. That way, all the goals I'm working on are in one spot. I urge you to try this. True, you'll have a couple of goals that will show up in both places, but that's no big deal. The main thing is: you can see all your goals at a glance.

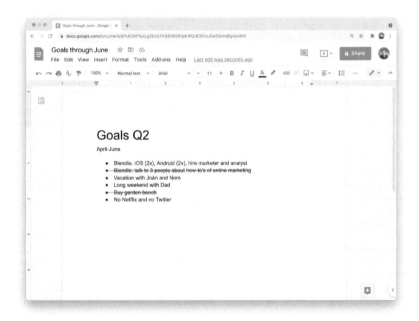

So you've written out your goals, you know why they matter to you, and you've defined when you'll be done. Great job! And now for making them happen . . .

The first step

Right now you may be looking at one of your goals without the faintest idea of where to start. I don't blame you, especially if it's a stretch goal. Just think back to my friends Herman and Sietske and their dream to live in a camper. Where do you even begin?

Actually, it's surprisingly simple. All you have to do is ask yourself one question: What's the first concrete step I could take on the way to this goal? It might be "Check listings of used campers for sale" or "Ask more experienced friends for tips." Remember when you turned your priorities into specific tasks in chapter 1 (p. 13)? Pursuing a goal works the same way. It's a matter of deciding what your next step could be and repeating this process until you cross the finish line.

Thought of a next step? Excellent. Before you do anything else, grab your calendar and schedule the time you'll need to complete it. That's how you can be sure to make this important (but likely not urgent) task a priority in your week.

After that, it's just a matter of buckling down. Close your email. Log out of Netflix. Take Facebook and Instagram off your phone (better yet, put your phone somewhere out of sight). Leave all those chores around the house for some other time, and *start*.

Having trouble getting going? Here are some more pointers:

- Make your first step even smaller so you can complete that first action within minutes. Let's say your goal is to master

Excel. Set a timer to watch a five-minute Excel tutorial on YouTube. Or if your goal is fitness related, start out with ten minutes of stretching exercises.

- After completing the first step, reward yourself. Give yourself a short break, a cup of coffee, or some other small treat.
- Remind yourself why this goal is so important to you. What do you hope to accomplish? Close your eyes and picture what it will be like when you reach this goal.

Lots of people have big plans; not everyone manages to bring them to fruition. The trick is to practice breaking down big ambitious endeavors into little doable tasks. You'll be amazed at how far this simple skill will take you and how much you'll accomplish.

Set realistic deadlines

A good goal also needs to have a deadline. Deadlines aren't something cooked up by stressed managers to antagonize staff. They have a proven effect on our work. Without deadlines, our attention strays to less important matters and we risk never reaching our goals at all.

Setting a long deadline may sound ideal, but it's not. See Parkinson's law: Work always expands to fill the time available. Give a complicated technical project a hard deadline of four weeks and I guarantee you'll be working up to the last day. It's the same on a small scale. Schedule two hours for a meeting and you'll fill 120 minutes. But a realistic deadline helps you get things done and keep moving.

Don't set too many goals at once

Another common pitfall is setting too many goals. Dividing your attention among lots of goals makes it less likely you'll achieve any of them. As I wrote earlier, my own ideal number is anywhere from four to seven. More than that and it gets hard to stay enthusiastic about them all. If you're unsure about a goal, my advice is to skip it this time around (or discuss it with your boss). If you wind up with extra time on your hands, you can always decide to throw another goal in.

Set aside time to evaluate

You can set new goals and add them to your overview any time you want. Once a quarter works best for me (as I'll discuss in the next chapter), but there's no particular rule here. What's important is making each goal a fixed part of your Friday recap (p. 97). It's the best way to track progress on your goals and write down next steps to take.

Another smart step I've learned to help me reach my goals is to actively involve others. Case in point: At my old job, we needed to hire staff before the quarter's end. I was really excited about this goal because the new hires would make our work better and more fun. This goal was also easy to measure, since it would be obvious if we'd hired new employees on time. So far, it checked all the boxes. But in the first few weeks, we made little progress toward our target. Sure, I'd jotted down some steps for myself to take, but we weren't coordinating our efforts. Selecting, approaching, and interviewing candidates was supposed to be a team effort and we all dropped the ball. In a way it was understandable, because this was a typical *important* and *not urgent* task, so it was the first thing to be postponed in the face of other work. Finally, our HR manager suggested changing tactics by doing weekly *check-ins*. We started holding a stand-up once a week with the whole team, to brief each other on what we'd done and what our next steps were. That really helped us pick up the pace because we were all counting on each other to accomplish a common goal. It goes to show that no matter how clearly you define your goals, or how enthusiastic you are about them, what *really* makes the difference is someone who looks over your shoulder and says, "Hey, how's it coming along? What have you done so far? What's next?"

A study at the Dominican University of California underscores the efficacy of teaming up this way.[4] Researchers there looked at different ways of working toward a goal. Turns out that participants who shared their goals with a friend scored significantly better at achieving them. They scored nearly 50 percent better than a control group that didn't share their goals. A group that also sent out weekly updates to a friend did even better: 77 percent better than the control group. This suggests sharing your progress is an excellent incentive for seeing a plan through, something we'll take a closer look at in chapter 7.

Don't be afraid to revise your goals

There are few things more frustrating than being confronted week in, week out with a goal that in hindsight isn't viable. This happened to me a few years ago when I set myself a big challenge. To hone my public speaking skills, I would give a presentation somewhere every month. The first two months got off to a flying start since I already had presentations scheduled. But then things stalled. March, April, and May passed in a flurry of other work and not a single presentation. My frustration grew. By June I was deftly sidestepping this goal in my weekly recap, and I didn't give any presentations for the rest of the year. That's a shame, because if I'd revised my goal to something more doable—like "Give four presentations this year" or "Email my presentation pitch to ten conferences"—I might have gotten a few more presentations in. Instead, I abandoned my original plan and topped out at two.

You may also experience this kind of frustration over goals agreed with your team or manager. When that happens, don't let yourself get discouraged; just approach those involved and broach the subject with them. By delving into the problem together, you might discover a whole different path to the original goal. Or agree on a different outcome that at least beats missing the target altogether.

Another time when it's smart to revise a goal is when you realize it's not clear enough. You and your coworkers, for instance, may have different interpretations of when a goal has been met. Clarifying matters, and getting everyone on the same page is key. Nothing drains energy like not really knowing what the target is or when you've reached it.

In this chapter you worked to discover what you like doing. It starts with putting together the three-piece puzzle of what drives you—those things you're passionate about and good at and that connect with what's important to you. And it turns out we're most effective when we have something to work toward. So set goals you're excited about. But even if your goals check all the boxes, you can take this approach to another level. How? By making plans for the year to come.

6. THE YEAR PLAN DAY
Making plans for the year in just one day

In chapter 4 you got acquainted with the Friday recap, where you look back over the past week and plan the next one. Most of us don't have time in our busy schedules to look much beyond that each week, let alone time to think about what we want for the coming year. That's where a *yearly* recap comes in. In this chapter I'll show you how to make the most of your year, by looking back on everything the year has brought and making plans for the year ahead.

It was Chris Guillebeau, an American author, globetrotter, and blogger, who sold me on the idea of an "annual review," which he describes on his blog. In 2014, I followed his steps for the first time to do a detailed review of my year.[1] I was so pleased with the results that I've been doing it ever since. To give you an idea of the ways it helped me:

- I spent time thinking about the kind of role I wanted at work, enrolled in a class to put me on that path, and reshaped the content of my job.
- I decided how I wanted to organize my team, what needed to change, and then made those changes.
- I came up with and launched a project to send out daily news-letters for a year.

- I made plans to exercise more, play the guitar more, and give more presentations.
- I decided to stop Netflix cold turkey, which freed up loads of time for other things.
- I organized outings with friends and family, like a day sailing with my mom. (She's a pro and, it turns out, a fantastic instructor!)

With an investment of a few hours, a yearly recap gives me results that last well into the next year. Can't argue with that math. So let's see how it works.

WHAT'S A YEARLY RECAP?

Like the Friday recap, your yearly recap is a time to look both back and forward. But that's where the similarities end. With a yearly recap, you think about completely different things. Instead of focusing on the short term, you take a long view. It's a time to consider the broad arc of the last twelve months and to dream unfettered about what you could do in the year ahead. The result? New insight into the past year, stronger memories, and a wealth of ideas for the time to come.

WHEN?

Doesn't matter. It's up to you. The best moment to look back on the past year and explore the next is whenever works for you. The main thing is to give yourself enough time. What works best for me is clearing my calendar for two days in a row. That way I can really take my time and enjoy remembering all that's happened. And then dream up new plans. I love those quiet days between Christmas and New Year's, but some people like to do their yearly recap some other time, like after getting back from a summer break. As I said, when you do it is up to you. And while it's certainly better if you can free up a good chunk of time, it's amazing how much you can get done in just one afternoon, if need be. Want to make the most of this chapter? Then stop reading for a moment, grab your calendar, and block at least half a day sometime this month for your Year Plan Day.

Before we get started on your Year Plan, here's what you can expect to get out of it:

- An overview of your year's highlights and lowlights
- Concrete goals for the next three months (I'll explain in a moment why the three-month horizon and not a whole year)
- A collection of ideas that you can dip into over the coming year

If this sounds pretty ambitious, don't worry. We'll take it one step at a time—starting with a look back.

A LOOK BACK

PLANNING YOUR YEAR

Step 1. Your year in review
YOUR CALENDAR
Your calendar is your rock. Makes sense to start there when reviewing the past year. We're going to start by scrolling through

it week by week. (If you haven't been using a calendar that long, scroll through the empty months and see if you can piece together what you were doing.) Write down any big event or noteworthy activity, along with the month, on one of two lists: we'll call them *highlights* and *lowlights*.

I like doing this digitally, but feel free to use whatever form you prefer—a notebook works great too. What things went well? What are you proud of? Add them to your list of highlights. What things could have gone better? Add them to your list of lowlights.

I love doing highlights and lowlights. It's great to reminisce while scrolling through the year's events, and I always come across a few things I'd completely forgotten about. I know someone who does step 1 as a family. It's great to see what highlights and lowlights kids come up with. Torben, age six, had a clear winner in the lowlights category: *When the cats got fleas (and the house did too)*.

If you want to get started quickly, I've put together a Year Plan Day template you're welcome to use. You can find it at gripbook. com/templates.

YOUR PICTURES

Now's the moment to make use of the fact that we take more pictures than ever. Take the time to look through your photos from the past year and add your thoughts about them to your lists of highlights and lowlights.

YOUR JOURNAL

Do you keep a journal? Flip through it. The blocks in your calendar won't tell you how you felt on a given day, so your journal can add valuable context. Or scroll through your social media posts. The more you've documented over the past year, even very briefly, the richer your material to review.

Step 2. Looking back on your goals

Looking back at the goals you set last year is a key part of a yearly recap. But the first time, you may not have clear-cut goals yet. That's no problem. You could try jotting down a few sentences about what you wanted to do this past year and why you did or didn't do it.

If you did set goals for yourself, then now's the time to look back at each of them. Go to a new page or fresh sheet of paper, and note each goal and whether you hit it. I like to jot down some thoughts while I'm at it about what went right (or wrong). Did I reach my original goal? Did I do everything I could to achieve it? Did I lose sight of the goal as the year progressed? Did I adapt my goal along the way? Or lose interest? Why? And what did I get out of the experience?

Now you've got three lists: the year's highlights, lowlights, and a review of your goals for the year.

Step 3. Category review

Now zoom in on specific aspects of your year, using whatever categories make sense for you. Here's the list I'm using. It keeps me from getting too focused on work alone. Feel free to pick from these categories or add new ones that work for you.

- Work
- Partner and home life
- Wider family
- Friends

- Health
- Spiritual life
- Skills
- Side projects
- Fun
- Giving
- Quitting
- Money—Income
- Money—Savings

Go to a fresh page and take a look at each category you're using. Think back over the past year and write down some observations about each one. Here are some questions to ask for each area of your life:

- What did I do?
- What didn't I do?
- What am I happy with and what am I not?
- What gave me loads of energy? What definitely didn't?

Work through the categories, jotting down your thoughts for each one. Take all the time you need. These valuable insights will help you in the year to come.

Here's what I wrote for one category:

- Friends:
  - Started a book club with some friends last year. Really great move. We did four interesting books.
  - Caught up with Jurgen on occasion, but not often enough. Would have liked to see him more.

It's like a job performance review . . . but without the boss

People underestimate how rewarding it can be to take a critical look at your own job performance. Since you have only yourself to answer to, there's no pressure to say what a manager wants to hear, and you can use your findings to inform the next steps you want to take. All at your own pace. That makes it a simple and straightforward way to give your personal development a boost. Plus, a proactive attitude often gets rewarded.

Step 4. Quarterly review

Now let's zoom out. Grab your highlights and lowlights from step 1, and this time write down your impressions of each quarter last year. Just a few sentences noting things that stuck with you. This helps you see whether any part of your year stands out from the rest. Is there anything that strikes you or surprises you? What makes you proud? A quick review could look something like this:

- Q1: Awesome vacation. But could have done a better job delegating my work beforehand. Took up cycling again! That went well thanks to a mild winter. Juggled three big projects. Completed two of them (new marketing campaign and new app launch) with stellar results. Would have liked to see more of my friends this Q. Built a new deck out back.
- Q2: Hardly got around to my goals at all this Q. Spent lots of time out on the new deck. Bliss! Worked hard.
- Q3: Made a fresh start on planning my work and spending less time on unimportant stuff. Made great progress. In hindsight,

wish I'd taken a week off this Q. Also would like to have read more books.

- Q4: Finally cleaned up the garage. (On my list for AGES.) Didn't feel at the top of my game this Q, was tired a lot and turned in early. Weather didn't help. Got a lot out of my manager's feedback. It felt good to apply some of her pointers right away.

These are valuable insights that can make a big difference when I make plans for the year to come.

Step 5. Reflect

This is the last step. Now that you've had a chance to recap the year's highlights and lowlights, the goals you set, your chosen categories, and had a quick look at all four quarters, try to sum up what you found in a couple of sentences. How did the past year go? Are you satisfied with your year? Were there any really fantastic things that happened? Or things that were difficult for you?

Your review will now look something like this:

A LOOK BACK

Highlights and lowlights

What went well? What am I happy with? What were the high points of my year?

- _____

- _____

- _____

What could have gone better? What am I not so happy about? What were the low points?

- _____

- _____

- _____

Goals

What was my goal? Did I reach it? Why or why not?

- Goal 1 _____

- Goal 2 _____

- Goal 3 _____

Categories

- Work _____

- Partner and home life _____

- Wider family _____

- Friends _____

Quarters

- Q1 _____

  _____

- Q2 _____

- Q3 _____

- Q4 _____

Now sum up your year

- This year was _____

Choose your own form

My sister makes little paintings for her yearly recap. She does her looking back in the form of a mind map, using colors, symbols, and little doodles to reflect on her year. I wish I had her talent, but I make do with a plain old list.

Looking back over your year does all kinds of useful things for you (like helping you do some things differently going forward, simply by taking the time to take stock). But it also lets you relive the highlights, some of which you're bound to have forgotten. Even in hard years, the Year Plan Day always makes me extra mindful of all that came into my life. I hope it will do the same for you.

BRAINSTORM

PLANNING YOUR YEAR

| LOOKING BACK | BRAINSTORMING | SETTING GOALS |

At this point, you *could* write down all the changes you've been wanting to make and call them your goals for next year. But that would be selling yourself short. I mean, if you're looking for a new car, you don't just buy the first one you spot because it's better than what you're driving now. Take the time to brainstorm a little and explore some more options. After all, these aren't just any old decisions. The choices you make now will affect a year of your life, so give yourself a chance to think them through.

The brainstorming phase of your yearly recap is about putting aside practical concerns and thinking *big*. The sky's the limit. Better yet, try not to limit yourself at all, and ignore any potential drawbacks for now. No need to confine yourself to the next twelve months either. You'll have a chance to judge your brain waves later.

To get the ball rolling, grab your review categories again. This time, you'll be writing down something you're excited about for each category. That's a great way to come up with your first rough ideas for next year. (What helps me here is rereading my brainstormed ideas from the year before. Many are still relevant or will prompt new ideas this time around.)

Ready to get started? Try out a brainstorming style that suits you. You could simply list what comes to mind for each category (as I do), or use Post-its for each individual idea, or turn it into artwork (as my sister does), or draw a mind map. Whether you opt for screen or paper is also up to you—what matters is to set your imagination free.

Below are some questions to get you thinking about each category. Feel free to use them as a jumping-off point and add your own. And one last tip: save this list of questions to use again next year.

BRAINSTORMING QUESTIONS

WORK

- Am I happy with my job?
- Do I want to keep doing this work?
- Do I want to work more?
- Do I want to work less?
- What kinds of projects do I want to do?
- What do I want to learn?
- What do I need to improve?
- What new thing do I want to start doing?
- What do I need to quit doing?
- Do I see myself in the same job three years from now?

- What's the most common feedback I get?
- What am I good at, and how can I build on that?

PARTNER AND HOME LIFE

If you're in a relationship, write down thoughts about your life with your partner (and your kids if you have them).

- What things do I want to do together?
- How do I feel about the amount of time we've spent together recently?
- What projects do I want to take on together?
- What would I like to change about our relationship?
- What do I want to start doing?
- What do I need to quit doing?

WIDER FAMILY

Make a list of family members you keep in touch with, and then write down your thoughts for each one.

- What could I offer them?
- What could I ask of them?
- Do I want to strengthen and deepen this relationship? If so, how do I want to do that?
- Which family members have I lost touch with recently? Do I want to do something about that? If so, what?

FRIENDS

Good friends are invaluable. They share in our happy moments and shore us up when times are tough. But with everything else going on in our lives, we sometimes lose sight of good friends.

Make a list of your close friends, then think about the same kinds of things you did for family members: *What can I offer them? What can I ask of them?* And also:

- Which friendships mean the most to me?
- Which friendships take the most out of me?
- Are there relationships I'd like to invest more in?
- Are there friends that have a negative effect on me?
- Are there friends I've lost touch with that I'd like to have back in my life?
- How do I envision my friendships growing?

HEALTH
- Am I getting enough sleep? Am I sleeping well?
- Am I eating a healthy and varied diet?
- Am I getting enough exercise?
- Am I happy with my daily routine? My morning, my evenings?
- How much do I drink?
- Am I addicted to anything? (Don't forget your phone, social media, or news here.)
- Do I see the dentist regularly?
- Am I mentally stable?

SPIRITUAL LIFE
- How well do I know myself?
- What role does spirituality play in my life?
- Would I like to have a more active spiritual life? (This can include organized religion, meditation, or mindfulness.)

SKILLS

- What would I like to learn to do?
- Which skills could help me get better at my job?
- Which skills would be fun to acquire?
- Is there a language I'd like to learn?
- A musical instrument I'd love to play?
- A sport I wish I were good at?

SIDE PROJECTS

Side projects are things you spend your spare time on, either to learn something new or earn some extra income. Things like part-time study, running a store on Etsy or eBay, taking a photography course, or writing a blog. Here are some questions you could ask:

- Do I have ideas for a side project I'd like to start?
- Which of my current side projects energize me most?
- What side projects do I want to continue?
- What side projects do I want to stop?
- Does it feel like my side projects are taking up too much time?
- What do my side projects tell me about my day job?

FUN

The first two years I did this brainstorm session, I didn't have a *Fun* category. That meant my plans for the next year were all on the earnest side. So don't skip this one. It's as vital as the others for fostering a full, well-rounded year and is guaranteed to bring good things into your life.

- What are some things I love to do in my spare time?

- What's going to be my big thing for recreation or relaxation this year?
- When I have a whole day ahead of me and no plans, what do I most enjoy doing?
- What would I most like to do more of?

GIVING

Consider *Giving* in the broadest sense. In previous editions of my yearly recap I linked giving exclusively to money. Then someone emailed me that my category *Money—Giving* was too limited, and I couldn't agree more. If you look at *Giving* in broader terms, all kinds of new possibilities open up.

- What can I contribute to the world? Think in terms of time, goods, or money.
- What skills can I teach someone else?
- Can I introduce people to others that will propel them forward in life or work?
- Would I be open to setting aside a fixed amount of money or time to give away?
- Reflect on how I spend my time. Is there a balance between what's good for me and what's good for others?

QUITTING

I added this category a couple of years back. It's often difficult to fit new things into your life without first scrapping some old things. The *Quitting* category can help.

- What's something that really saps my energy?
- What responsibilities of mine would be better passed on to someone else?

- What's something I do but aren't really excelling at and might be better off letting go?

MONEY—INCOME

- Is there anything in the near term that will seriously impact my income?
- What would I like my future income to be?
- How much do I need?
- How do my spending habits stack up?

MONEY—SAVINGS

- What are my savings goals, and why?
- Are there any big expenses in my future to start saving for? Things like the birth of a child, college tuition, or buying a house?
- What percentage of my income do I save?
- Do I need to start saving for retirement? Or change my investments?

SET CONCRETE GOALS

PLANNING YOUR YEAR

| LOOKING BACK > BRAINSTORMING > SETTING GOALS |

After enjoying a look back over your year and brainstorming for new ideas, you've come to the final step: setting goals. And I'll make this super easy for you. Rather than coming up with goals for the whole year, you only need to worry about the next three months.

Why three months? First off, I've found that a year is just too long when it comes to formulating concrete goals. You lose sight of them somewhere along the way or they feel like such a huge burden that it's easier to just keep putting them off. What's more, making choices for a full year is pretty tricky. On the flip side, a month is too short. Just when you start making real progress, it's time to wrap things up. Quarterly goals are the happy medium that offer by far the best odds of success. I've seen that in my own work, and for the people I work with too.

And don't bother setting specific deadlines for each goal. Your deadline is the end of the quarter. One less thing to worry about!

Step 1. Set goals by category

Now we're going to get to work with the results of your brainstorming session. For each category, choose one to three wishes that you'd like to turn into a goal for next quarter. How? Based on your enthusiasm. You can use your answers about your mission, passion, and skills from the last chapter to help.

My list might look like this:

WORK
- Something with presenting
- Become the owner of a key project

WIDER FAMILY
- Phone my mom on a regular basis

FITNESS
- Run a race
- Maybe start swimming?

As enthusiastic as I am about these goals (criterion 1 of a good goal, see p. 126 in chapter 5), they're not yet *measurable* (criterion 2). So I'll first translate this list into measurable goals, because that's just as crucial for meeting them. See chapter 5 for more on how to set and meet goals.

Now my list of goals for next quarter looks like this:

Goals for April through June

WORK

- Read a book on presenting
- Give one presentation and get feedback from two coworkers
- Become the owner of the new company website project

WIDER FAMILY

- Phone Mom once a week

FITNESS

- Run a 10k race
- Swim once a week

Okay, okay, I can hear you thinking: Did I really need to make a goal out of calling my mom? Won't that turn it into a chore? Not at all. Plus, your goals are up to you. For me, making a goal of setting aside time for friends and family just works better. How do I know? Because the results—a weekend trip with my dad, a day sailing with my mom—turned out to be highlights of my year. So give it a try. You can change your mind at any time. What have you got to lose?

At this stage you may feel hesitant to make some goals 100 percent final. Maybe you want to get your boss's input on one of them first. Don't let that hold you back. I have yet to meet a manager who's opposed to measurable goals! So with that in mind, go ahead and make your goals as concrete as you can.

Step 2. Final check

Now you have a set of concrete, challenging, measurable goals for the next three months. You may have five, fifteen, or even twenty. Better to have fewer goals and achieve all of them than to bite off more than you can chew. Less is more. You can pare down your list using these questions:

- Will you be working on the things that are really important to you next quarter?
- Are there other events or activities next quarter that didn't come up in your brainstorming session but will require a significant chunk of time? If your goal is to go swimming every week but you've got a three-week hiking trip coming up, now's the time to adjust that goal.
- Do your goals challenge you enough? Do you have a good balance between goals and stretch goals?

Step 3. Outline the next three quarters

After setting your first-quarter goals, it's a good idea to lay out the broad strokes of the rest of your year. Don't worry about filling it in yet—this is purely a rough outline. Maybe you already have some goals on the horizon, like a major campaign at work or a DIY project at home. Or an important event coming up, like a big trip or a new baby. Run through your brainstorming notes again to find these sorts of goals-in-the-making. Your rough outline of the year might look something like this:

Q2

- Clean out attic
- Hire intern
- Vacation at the beach?

Q3

- Kick off our company's big partnership with the city
- I'd like to take more day trips to the coast this year

Q4

- Make more time for family over the holidays?

As you can see, my outline for the next three quarters throws together personal projects, vague ideas, and a reminder to spend more time with family at the end of the year. That last item was an insight gleaned from reflecting on last year. Though nothing's set in stone yet, this plan contains a couple of clear guideposts to mark my intentions. Those will be useful later on when I'm ready to set more concrete goals for my second, third, and fourth quarters. More on that in a moment.

With this last step, you've completed your plan for the coming year. Can't wait to get started? Great.

ACHIEVING THIS QUARTER'S GOALS

Setting goals is one thing. Actually achieving them is something different. Over the years, I noticed a link between the goals I achieved and how often I'd been reminded of them—no matter who did the reminding. And that taught me an important lesson: to give yourself the best odds of achieving goals, they have to keep crossing your radar.

What's needed is a simple way to keep sight of quarterly goals. The great news is we have the perfect tool already: the Friday recap (chapter 4). I add this quarter's goals to my personal checklist (p. 103). That way I'll see these goals and—more important—come up with follow-up actions every week.

Another thing that really helps me is to break goals down into bite-sized steps. I can do a little each week, and it's easier to fit into my schedule.

If you want to be even more effective, it can be incredibly useful to find someone who'll help you stick to your goals. You can start simple. Agree with someone to exchange a weekly email summarizing what progress you've made toward your goals. In the next chapter, I'll give you tips on how having a partner in crime can help.

End of quarter

At the end of the quarter, it's time to set new goals for next quarter. This is like the big brainstorming session you did for the whole year, except quicker and easier because you've already done most of the brainwork.

Here are the steps I take to plan a new quarter. They're basically a condensed version of the ones I showed you earlier in this chapter. Feel free to use my template, which you can find at gripbook.com/templates.

A QUICK LOOK BACK
- Step 1: Write down your highlights and lowlights from the past three months (p. 144).
- Step 2: Check your quarterly goals and cross off those you've reached (p. 145).

- Step 3: For each category you pick, jot down one or two lines on how the past quarter went (p. 145).
- Step 4: Sum up the quarter as a whole in a couple of sentences (p. 146).

SETTING NEW GOALS
- Step 1: Grab the notes you made during your yearly brainstorming session and your outline for the next three quarters, and use them to set new goals for next quarter (p. 153).
- Step 2: Double-check if these goals are your most important work right now (p. 156).
- Step 3: Scan your outline for the rest of the year. Has anything changed? Update your outline.
- Step 4 (optional): Share your goals with a good friend or coworker.

You'll see that doing these little quarterly reviews makes your next yearly recap that much easier, because you've summed up everything in four chunks already.

So go ahead and give a yearly recap a try. Reserve some time for it as soon as you can. You'll be amazed by the new insight you'll gain, and the greater sense of direction it brings to your work and your life.

But we all know sticking to your plans can be tricky. My solution? Recruit someone who'll help you along and keep you on the right track. Time for a partner in crime.

7. NEXT-LEVEL ENCOURAGEMENT

A weekly session with your partner in crime

J. R. R. Tolkien, author of the legendary *Lord of the Rings*, once said of fellow writer and friend C. S. Lewis: "The unpayable debt that I owe to [Lewis] was not 'influence' as it is ordinarily understood but sheer encouragement. He was for long my only audience. Only from him did I ever get the idea that my 'stuff' could be more than a private hobby."[1]

We all need encouragement. Self-motivation takes you only so far, and that's especially true in trying times or with big projects. That's why I make sharing work a priority, wherever I work—whether in weekly meetings I led at my agency, in the daily stand-ups we did at Blendle, or the online group of entrepreneurs I'm a part of now. These sessions are not only fun and interesting, but when people come together and share what they're working on, it's incredibly inspiring and encouraging.

And so I came up with another way to find encouragement. In 2014, I started doing weekly Skype sessions with Derk, a former business associate who's about my age. Our chats, in which we ask about each other's work and life, fuel both of us to go the extra mile. And they've become a regular highlight of my week.

A weekly recap as we set up in chapter 4 is a time to get things straight, check to make sure nothing slipped through the cracks this week, and then make a plan for the next. But to make this work, you have to keep on top of it. Your weekly recap doesn't talk back, and if you wanted to, you could easily sidestep the tough stuff.

Having a good *accountability partner*—or what I like to call a partner in crime—makes that kind of evasion hard. A partner reminds you of your resolutions, offers new insight, encourages you in what you're good at, and points out where you have room to grow. You give them a green light to tell you what they see— even things you'd rather not hear.

This weekly chat with your partner in crime doesn't replace your weekly recap. You want to do both. Where your recap orders the chaos and maps out your new week, an accountability session centers on sharing your plans with a person who can give you critical feedback. And you do the same for them.

But first things first: How do you find the perfect partner in crime?

Finding a partner in crime

When I tell people about my accountability sessions, their first reaction tends to be surprise. The second is: "I have no idea who I could do that with. Isn't that asking a lot of someone?"

Don't worry about imposing, because you both benefit. This is a dialogue; your input is just as valuable to them. Here are some pointers for finding that perfect partner:

- You want someone you trust and feel comfortable enough with to discuss a wide range of issues. Derk and I didn't know each other all that well, so our first exchanges focused mainly on our jobs. Once we got going, we began sharing our ambitions and dreams beyond work.

- You want a good listener. These sessions have exponentially higher impact if your partner gives you the space to tell your story. (Also, learn to be a good listener. More on that in chapter 9.)
- You want someone who energizes you. You should come out of each session buoyed by fresh energy to go after your goals.
- You want someone who's not afraid to tell you the truth, who's willing to be straight with you.

I know this first step can feel a little daunting. But don't let that hold you back. There's sure to be someone in your network who checks all the boxes. Take a look at your LinkedIn connections, for starters. Or is there a former classmate, business partner, or coworker from a different team or city who may be up for trying a few accountability sessions? Think of it as a trial period. If it doesn't work out, you two can always leave it at that.

Found a potential candidate? Once they're on board, it's time to organize your first session.

The first session

This step's easy: pick a time to talk. During this first session you'll agree on how to structure your discussions. Here are some questions you'll definitely want to address:

- What's the setup for our sessions? What will we cover? (I'll share our standard questions in a moment.)
- Which topics do we want to discuss? Is anything off limits?

- How often will we meet?
- What do we expect from each other?
- What do we hope to get out of these sessions?
- How long is our trial period?

For these sessions to have the biggest impact, you need time to feel each other out. After the first session, think carefully about whether this partner is right for you. The way Derk and I did this was by agreeing we'd have three sessions and then decide if it was a good fit.

How do I do an accountability session?

Before jumping into how the session itself works, I'd like to share some of our findings first. I hope the lessons we've learned over the years could help make your sessions better, faster.

TIMING

Like me, Derk is busy most evenings. Since we wanted to meet at a set time, we settled on a fixed weekday morning before work. That's also ideal for another reason. Because one or both of us will usually have another appointment soon afterward, we're forced to keep an eye on the time. We connect by video call since we're almost always in different cities.

LENGTH

Whenever you decide to meet—mornings, during the day, or in the evening—it's good to keep an eye on the clock. Setting a time limit ensures you stay focused on the topic at hand and cut to the chase. Derk and I set aside thirty minutes for our weekly sessions, giving us each fifteen minutes to talk. Initially

we took turns asking questions, but that left us both too focused on our own answers. Dividing the time in half fixed that
problem.

TAKING NOTES

We've noticed we listen much more actively if we take notes.
When my partner in crime's talking, I sum up his points in a
shared Google Doc so he can follow along in real time. He can
then concentrate on telling his story and sees instantly if his
message is getting across. Another benefit of taking notes is that
we have an archive of our conversations. That comes in handy
when looking back on the year.

PREPARATION IS KEY

In every session, we each run down a fixed list of questions
(more on that later). Early on we noticed we got more out of it
if we thought about our answers beforehand, so now we write
them down for ourselves before each session. That preparation
helps us to be more precise, and it also makes it easier to be attentive to your partner's feedback, because you're not preoccu-
pied with how you'll answer the next question. If you feel you
could be getting more out of your sessions, check to see if you're
both doing the prep work.

FREQUENCY

My partner and I talk every week, but that wasn't how we started
out. Our first sessions were every other week. By the time the
next session rolled around, we'd let our planned actions slide,
reshuffled our priorities, and forgotten what we'd wanted to improve. Now, whenever we're forced to skip a week, I find myself

feeling less driven and focused. Turns out weekly sessions are far more effective for us. See if the same is true for you.

The format

You know how a clear agenda makes meetings run more smoothly? The same goes for accountability sessions. If you don't draw up a solid agenda in advance, there's a real risk you'll spend the whole session going off on tangents. And while a little socializing is welcome, especially when working from home, you also want to make the most of your time together. That's why Derk and I stick to a fixed set of questions that keeps our discussion moving along. Here's that list, which I'll walk you through below:

1. What quarterly goal are you working on?
2. How did you do on the actions you set for last week?
3. What went well last week and why?
4. What could you have done better?
5. How are you keeping things in balance?
6. How can you be a better partner and parent?
7. What concrete actions will you take next week?

We've made a point of wording these questions so they'll lead us to our next action. "How's your relationship with your partner?" might be interesting to talk about, but it doesn't trigger you to act. "How can you be a better partner?" takes you straight to things you can do. And that's exactly what you want: a friendly push to start making changes. Simple tweaks like that can help take your dialogue to another level. So try out different forms of questioning and see what works for the two of you.

My partner and I also regularly check whether our questions do what we want them to do. If not, we update our list. But the basic formula doesn't change. We look back, we consider whether our actions are in line with our goals, and then we look ahead to the coming week. If we start repeating ourselves from week to week, it means a particular question isn't very effective. That's a sign we need to rethink our list.

WHAT QUARTERLY GOAL ARE YOU WORKING ON?

In chapter 6, we looked at how to make a proactive plan for the year ahead. That helps you set goals each quarter—goals you'll then look at each week in your weekly recap. Together, these elements keep you focused on what you want to do.

You can make certain you don't lose sight of your goals by building them into your accountability sessions. After all, the more you're reminded of your goals, the more likely you are to meet them.

Derk and I decided to open our sessions with the question *Which quarterly goal are you working on?* That forces us to decide which goal is our current top priority. Right off, my answer tells me what to block the most time for this coming week. Meanwhile, my accountability partner notes down the actions I plan to take toward my chosen goal.

Don't have quarterly goals yet? No problem. Try starting your sessions with the *one thing* question: *What's the one thing you want to focus on most next week?*

HOW DID YOU DO ON YOUR ACTIONS FOR LAST WEEK?

We use this question to check if we tackled the actions we'd set for last week. If not, it's nothing to be ashamed of. Happens to the best of us. The idea is to discuss why with your accountability partner and find a fresh angle to try again next week.

WHAT WENT WELL LAST WEEK, AND WHY?

This sounds like a simple question—until you get to the *why* at the end. It's easy to talk about jobs well done, but harder to consider *how* you did them. Think back and ask: *Why does it make you particularly happy or proud? What was your contribution?* To come up with a good answer, you need to be very precise. An easy answer might be: "I aced a big meeting," but that's much less informative than: "I'm happy I managed to free up extra time on Tuesday to prepare for a big meeting on Wednesday. The meeting went off without a hitch and I'm excited about the outcome." The second answer pinpoints where you made smart choices. That's what you want.

WHAT COULD YOU HAVE DONE BETTER?

For me, this is the most important question of the session, because it's from my mistakes that I always learn the most. It can be tempting to give an easy answer and move on. Resist! Take the time to really think about this one. I like to scroll through my calendar before each session to refresh my memory. Or if you keep a journal, that can help too. Case in point: exploring this question made me realize that weekends with back-to-back activities were a huge source of frustration for me. Now that I'm aware of that, it's just a matter of making sure I don't overload my weekends. And my partner in crime keeps me sharp by asking me about this periodically.

HOW ARE YOU KEEPING THINGS IN BALANCE?

This is a question my partner and I added to our list some time back. We noticed we were losing ourselves in our hectic lives and not taking time to look after ourselves. Not enough sleep, no real downtime, and too much crammed into our evenings—we both knew things had to change. Asking this question each week makes us stop and think about the pace we're setting and whether it's healthy and sustainable.

HOW CAN YOU BE A BETTER PARTNER AND PARENT?

Since starting out, our sessions have become more personal. One thing that's important to both of us is being good partners. By now Derk and I know each other well enough to share that facet of our lives. Putting this question on our weekly agenda gets us to actively think about these relationships. And now that we both have kids, this question means we reflect on our roles as fathers on a weekly basis.

WHAT CONCRETE ACTIONS WILL YOU TAKE NEXT WEEK?

This question is at the heart of our sessions (along with *What could you have done better?*). It's where we sum up all the actions raised so far. Derk and I could just note them down separately for ourselves, but knowing me, I'd be lucky to finish even half of what I planned. We've found that formulating and writing action items down together, in our shared session notes, works much better.

When prepping for a session, you'll already start to think of follow-ups for your other quarterly goals. Now's a good time to run through those actions together briefly, making them part of your list of action points. After the session, take a moment to slot those actions into your calendar and to-do list. There's bound to be some overlap with tasks you'd already set in your weekly recap—so much the better. Talking with your partner in crime will often spark fresh insights. In that case, you may want to shift some things around, so take the time to make those changes. On the other hand, if your schedule for the week was perfect as is, that's also good to know. Either way, adding all these actions to your system right after your session helps ensure you'll actually get around to them.

Between sessions, Derk and I send each other progress updates. Otherwise it can be tempting to postpone those critical actions, even when doing them will only take a moment. Our messages aren't intended to check up on each other, but to help encourage us both to press ahead. That keeps us on track. And it feels great to share our achievements! *How* you encourage each other is of course up to you. The key is to agree on what you expect from one another, what feels comfortable, and what works.

Pitfalls

Like everything else in life, your accountability sessions are a work in progress. Refining them just takes some practice. But you can get a jump on things by learning from some of the mistakes we've made.

1. NOT ASKING ENOUGH CRITICAL QUESTIONS

The first answer you get (or give) is almost never the full answer. So the quality of your sessions leans heavily on smart, constructive follow-up questions. It all hinges on staying critical. That's the power of these sessions, but it also puts you in the hot seat.

After a while, you'll learn to expect what your partner will ask about. If they too easily take an answer at face value, don't hesitate to point that out. The same applies to you. When your partner is the one sharing, give positive, constructive feedback. The idea isn't to second-guess them, but to ask probing questions to shine a light on their answers and boost their motivation.

2. NOT FOLLOWING UP ON PLANNED ACTIONS

Writing down actions is important, but if you don't review your progress in the next session, it's all too easy to let them fall by the wayside. That's why if something doesn't pan out—regardless of the reason—your partner should feel free to say, "It's a shame you weren't able to do X." That opens the door to talking about taking it up again and how else you could try doing it.

My accountability sessions with Derk have already paid off in so many ways, helping me successfully relocate, experiment with new avenues at work, and deepen relationships with friends and family—just to name a few. And I'm not alone in experiencing the incredible power of talking with a partner in crime about what matters most to you. I've heard loads of enthusiastic stories from others. So the only question left at the close of this chapter is, *What are you waiting for?*

CHEAT SHEET FOR PART 2

What gets you out of bed? (p. 115)

- Write down your mission: What's important to you?
- Write down your passion: What do you love doing?
- Write down your skills: What are you good at?
- What do you want to achieve that fits your mission, passion, and skills?
- What concrete goals could help you do that?

Setting goals (p. 126)

- Ask yourself: *Am I excited about this goal?*
- *How will I know when I've reached the goal?*

Achieving your goals (p. 131)

- Make sure you have a clear next step, and make it as small as you can.
- Give yourself a realistic deadline.
- Don't tackle too many goals at once. Not making progress? Get rid of some.
- Schedule times to evaluate your goals.
- If your interest starts flagging, revise your goals.

Your Year Plan Day

A look back (p. 139)

- Go through your calendar week by week and start a list of highlights and lowlights.
- Look at your pictures and social media posts from the past year and add to your list.
- Flip through your journal and add any highlights and lowlights to your list.
- Did you set goals this past year? Note whether you reached each one.
- Look back on your year using whatever categories make sense for you: Work, Partner and Home Life, Wider Family, Friends, Health, Spiritual Life, Skills, Side Projects, Fun, Giving, Quitting, Money—Income, Money—Savings.
- Jot down your thoughts about each quarter.
- Write a couple of sentences on the year as a whole.

A look ahead (p. 153)

- Look ahead using whatever categories you'd like: Work, Partner and Home Life, Wider Family, Friends, Health, Spiritual Life, Skills, Side Projects, Fun, Giving, Quitting, Money—Income, Money—Savings.
- Brainstorm dreams and ideas for each category you choose.
- Formulate two or three measurable goals per category for the next three months.
- Think you'll reach your goals? If not, pare down your list until it feels doable.
- Check that you'll be spending next quarter working on what matters most to you.

- Anything big coming up that could conflict with your plan (a long trip, big project, or new baby)?
- Take a step back and ask: *Am I challenging myself enough?*
- Make a rough outline for the next three quarters.

Sessions with your partner in crime

Finding a partner in crime (p. 162)

- Find someone you trust.
- Find a good listener.
- Find someone who energizes you.
- Find someone who's not afraid to be straight with you.

The first session (p. 163)

- What's the setup for our sessions?
- Which topics do we want to discuss? Is anything off limits?
- How often will we meet?
- What do we expect from each other?
- What do we hope to get out of these sessions?
- How long is our trial period?

The questions (p. 166)

- What quarterly goal are you working on?
- How did you do on the actions you set for last week?
- What went well last week and why?
- What could you have done better?
- How are you keeping things in balance?
- How can you be a better partner and parent?
- What concrete actions will you take next week?

PART 3

GRIP

AND YOUR

LIFE

n the last few chapters we've already taken things up a notch by using ordinary tools in new ways. We made your calendar your rock, you built a backup brain to free up your mind, took charge of your inbox, started working with a net by doing a Friday recap, held a Year Plan Day, set goals you'll actually do, and tried your first sessions with a partner in crime. Nice job. So what's next?

Part 3 of this book is going to help you really cruise along. It's completely different from what we covered in the previous chapters. To take things to the next level, we'll zoom in on *you*. Part 3 covers the art of being yourself, only better—listening better, learning to think more strategically, getting better advice, and finally, thinking big while starting small. In short, get ready to up your game.

8. BEING YOURSELF, BUT BETTER
Changing your behavior and self-image

You have your workweek squared away. You have a grip on your work, your goals, and your motivation. Now's the perfect time to work on yourself. What can you do to keep becoming a better you? To hone your skills? And how can you do that without burning out?

To answer these questions, let's start with your self-image. How do you see yourself? Are you sloppy? Or a stickler for details? Do you find it easy or hard to adapt to change? Are you an easygoing person or the cautious type who needs to get comfortable before opening up?

You might say these characteristics are what it means to be you—that being sloppy or averse to change is part of your makeup. "I work slowly because I'm a perfectionist" or "I'm chaotic so I'm terrible at making plans." We're all made differently—that's true enough. Even so, if experience has taught me anything, it's that we have more control over how we feel and behave than we tend to assume. Turns out we can steer even the most fundamental character traits in the directions in which we want to grow. Complicated? Not at all. You just have to know where to start.

In chapter 3, on email, I touched on how addiction works. With addiction there's always a trigger, a habit, and a reward. This cycle perpetuates both negative addictions and positive ones. Your behavior can be modeled almost exactly the same way.

Self-image is the story we tell about ourselves. It's the things you say to yourself and others, and this commentary serves as a trigger for how you act. So, if you tell yourself every day that you're clumsy, you'll constantly see aspects of your behavior that affirm your clumsiness.

Environments can also reinforce particular behaviors. Case in point: I noticed I wasn't showing my creative side in meetings and was contributing very few ideas. It dawned on me that this had nothing to do with the ideas themselves and everything to do with my behavior. In meetings, I was often surrounded by people who were quick on their feet and comfortable throwing out ideas left and right. Meanwhile I listened attentively to understand what they meant. No one asked for my input. Everyone was focused on sharing their own views. They assumed that my silence meant I had nothing to add. Each time this happened was another mark against my sense of my own creativity. That influenced my self-image, which reinforced my behavior, and so on.

Unintentionally, I evolved a mindset that continually confirmed my lack of creativity. With time, it became a circuit imprinted in my brain. Not only did I start to believe I wasn't any good at creative thinking; I even heard myself saying, "I'm not creative." In other words, it had become part of my personality.

It's important to realize that this cycle is super addictive. Even when that story in your head doesn't quite feel right, the repeated confirmation fools you into believing it all makes sense. Your behavior seems in sync with your personality. And our brains love things that seem to make sense. If you think back to chapter 1, this is classic *system 1* thinking: Thinking something you already believe takes less energy than changing the pattern.

But there's good news. As soon as you understand *how* your brain's leading you astray, you can break the vicious circle. The same process that imprinted that pattern can now be used to reverse it.

ADJUSTING YOUR BEHAVIOR

Let's say I start changing my behavior. From now on, I'll work out my ideas beforehand so I'm ready to speak up and stand by them. I'll tap into the energy of people listening to my story. I'll experience how much I enjoy sharing my creative ideas. Sure, I'll still get critical input, but that just proves my ideas are being taken seriously. Gradually, the story I tell myself will start to shift, from "I'm not creative" to "Given a little time, I come up with some pretty great ideas." And my behavior will conform to this new story about myself.

Sound delusional? Well, it's not. In fact, that's exactly what happened with me.

How about another example. I have a friend who's transformed over the last six years. You wouldn't recognize him if you hadn't seen him in the meantime. Six years ago, he was a smoker and the opposite of athletic. Then he decided to change the story in his head, from "I'm not athletic" to "I'm a runner." That's quite the shift. And a story that ingrained doesn't rewrite itself. It takes effort. My friend started training—cautiously at first, then more seriously. These days he's in peak form and has healthy habits, with multiple marathons and even triathlons under his belt. The positive energy sparked by modifying his behavior not only transformed his story but is affirmed by everyone around him. When they remark on his fitness, he doesn't just say, "Yeah,

I run a lot," but asserts, "I'm a runner." He's living proof that we can take a characteristic that might feel alien to us and turn it into new behavior and an integral part of our self-image.

The takeaway? If you want to rewrite your story, then ignore what you've always said about yourself and start changing your behavior in small steps. Like this:

THE STORY ABOUT YOURSELF	WHAT CAN YOU DO?
I'M NOT ORGANIZED	Think of one area where you could be slightly more organized. There's no quicker way to internalize a new habit than by practicing it regularly. It could be as simple as putting up a key rack and getting used to hanging up your keys first thing when you come home. Now, you're no longer "not organized."
I DON'T HAVE ANY CREATIVE IDEAS	Buy a notebook to keep with you at all times so you can jot down every idea that pops into your head—even the duds.
	Set aside five minutes daily to brainstorm some topic. Jot down everything that occurs to you.
I CAN'T WRITE	Start a journal. No one else will see it; no one else will read it. Write one paragraph in it every day.
	Start a blog and write something there from time to time. Use a pseudonym if you want.
	Spend a little extra time polishing your emails.
I'M SLOPPY	Pick a routine action and throw in a tiny new habit that forces you to be tidier from now on. I know that if I dump my clothes beside the bed in the evening, I won't pick them up. So I've relocated my sloppiness to the hallway, forcing me to pick up my clothes and drop them in the hamper first thing in the morning, because they're literally in my way.

THE STORY ABOUT YOURSELF	WHAT CAN YOU DO?
I'M A PUSHOVER	Don't automatically say, "Yes." Ask the other person to explain their request again, giving you more time to consider.
	Ask for more time to think about a proposal so you can weigh the pros and cons. It's only reasonable not to want to make big decisions on the spur of the moment.

I don't mean to suggest that everything is fixable. Our futures can't be wholly engineered simply by tweaking our actions. But as I hope these examples show, you have the power to change more than you might think. And it's worth a shot, right?

Of course, some behavioral patterns are entrenched and deeply rooted in your past. If there's a cycle you can't overcome on your own, then talk to a professional.

I believe we can all benefit from talking to a psychologist. When I went looking for tools and techniques to help me collaborate better, I booked a couple of sessions with an occupational therapist. As confronting as it was, our sessions gave me some fascinating insight into my own head. I urge everyone who's able to try it sometime.

Ingredients of successful behavioral change:
- Modify your behavior in the smallest possible increments so it's nearly impossible to resist.
- Focus on one element at a time rather than trying to change a number of behaviors at once. Transformation takes loads of energy, so starting small will boost your odds of success.

- If you want to change a behavior, it's useful to know when and where it occurs. Is there a pattern? If so, you'll know when to be on guard.
- Can you hitch the new behavior to a fixed time or activity? Do two things together long enough and it's habit-forming. Add "floss" to your nightly "brush teeth before bed," for instance, and your brain will start to automatically link the activities. All it takes is repetition.
- Identify the biggest stumbling blocks on the road to your new behavior. Counter each stumbling block ahead of time using the *if this, then that* rule. So: "*If* it rains, *then* I'll put on my windbreaker and go running anyway." It stops you from reaching for excuses whenever obstacles pop up.
- Advertise your new behavior to the people around you or make them accomplices in your plans. For instance, tell friends that you don't lose your keys anymore since placing them in a fixed spot, or announce you'll be writing down everything agreed at meetings from now on so you won't forget anything. This changes the story in your own mind and in the minds of people around you. If you're lucky, they may even cheer you on.

The Seinfeld Method

Stand-up comedian Jerry Seinfeld came up with his own strategy for taking control of his behavior. He called it "Don't break the chain." He hung a big calendar on his wall and made a deal with himself to only put an X through days when he wrote new material. Just one joke was enough. Not breaking that chain of daily Xs turned into his motto. Seinfeld's method is an incredibly effective way to internalize a behavior change.

HEALTHY SELF-DEVELOPMENT

None of us is ever done growing. But how do you stay sane in the face of constant pressure to do better? You may remember back in the introduction to this book I said I'm allergic to people urging us to take it easy and stop working so hard. That's not something you'll hear me say. But I do believe in taking a healthy approach to self-development and respecting your own limits. In the last few years I've discovered there's a smarter way to nurture my own drive and ambition.

Every one of us is fueled by three forces: our energy, external expectations, and our own expectations. The question is, at what point are you overstepping your limits? To answer that, let's take a closer look at this three-force model.

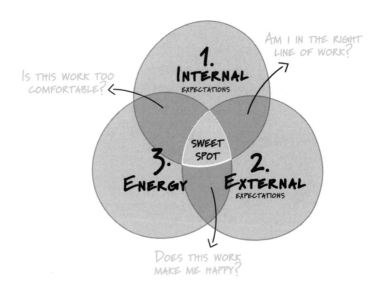

Force 1. Your internal expectations

Your own expectations are that inner voice that keeps prodding you to reach for the growth and development opportunities awaiting you. Steering by this internal compass is fine as long as (1) it's compatible with the external expectations of you (see diagram) *and* (2) your own growth and improvement efforts energize you, and don't just suck energy.

If you wind up solely in the *internal expectations* circle, with no overlap, it's an indication your own expectations are sky-high. Those expectations aren't coming from outside (circle 2) and aren't energizing you (circle 3). This puts you in the danger zone. You're placing unrealistically high demands on yourself and they're draining your energy.

Something I do to help me catch this kind of behavior is what's known as the "out-of-body experience." Pretend you're floating outside yourself and looking down on yourself working or relaxing. Picture yourself sitting at your desk, in a chair, on the couch. What's your opinion of this person? Are their aspirations for growth healthy and realistic? What would you tell them?

Some years back, there was a long period when I produced and posted daily videos on YouTube. Doing the out-of-body exercise made me realize nobody else was asking me to record and edit videos every single day. The only person with this absurd expectation was *me*.

An *out-of-body* experience—even an imagined one—almost always opens up refreshing new perspectives. And they might just lead you to conclude it's time to rethink your ambitions for growth or improvement.

Force 2. External expectations

There's no reason to mindlessly conform to what the outside world expects of you—or what you think it expects. Same goes for the opinions of strangers about who you are and what you do. They're best ignored. But beyond this group there are some external expectations you can't ignore. Like those of your boss or your coworkers, your friends, and your family.

If the expectations others have for you are higher than your own, it's easy to feel discouraged. The mismatch guarantees stress. And not the kind of stress that makes you the best you can be, but the dangerous kind that can burn you out.

Are external expectations on the job weighing you down? Is work taking more out of you than it's giving back? Anytime you're overburdened by pressures coming at you from outside, it deserves serious attention. First of all, take your sense of those expectations with a giant grain of salt. Nine times out of ten, expectations you perceive aren't consistent with *actual* expectations. This is where things tend to go wrong, especially if those expectations were never clearly articulated in the first place. In that case, I recommend talking to your manager. But first, get straight for yourself what you think the expectations are. Be concrete. When do you feel the most pressure? Are you really expected to reply within five minutes if your boss emails you on a Saturday? Do colleagues really expect you to have instant answers to every complex question raised in meetings?

If the outside expectations truly are unrealistic and it's all just too much, then it's time to ask if things can be taken down a notch. After all, no one wants you to be out of the running for months with a debilitating burnout. A realistic set of duties balancing things you're good at with the right learning curve will

Ask for specifics

Want to have an informative discussion? Start by asking good questions. Better questions yield better answers and more useful insights. And that doesn't just go for work conversations, but for personal ones too.

When I'm looking for information so I can make a decision or tackle a problem, I find it helps to aim my questions at three specific aspects: significance, situation, and emotion. Asking about specifics gives you more concrete takeaways.

Significance. What was the rationale behind the choices made? Try to find out what steps led up to these choices and what they were meant to achieve.

Situation. Things don't happen in a vacuum. Context can be critical. Knowing that, try to tease out the circumstances surrounding the person's decision. What factors influenced the choices they made? What factors influenced the results? Are there factors you're unfamiliar with? Ask questions to find out more.

Emotion. Now look at the effects of this person's choices. How do they feel about the new situation? How are they dealing with those effects? Are these feelings new? Or have they changed over time?

These three aspects can help you structure your discussions. What also helps me is to write down what I want to know in advance—especially if my research question is broad, like with my online marketing example. Better yet, make a detailed list of your questions. That keeps you focused on what matters and lets you listen to the answers instead of wondering what to ask next.

To get the conversation going, you can ask questions like: "We're planning to do X and I understand you have some experience with that. Could you tell me what your strategy was, and why?" or "I'm considering getting software package Y and know you're a big fan. Could you tell me what you like about it?"

When I was looking for information about online marketing, my question was: "I'm curious about your most successful online marketing channels. What worked best for you, and what fell flat?"

And don't forget to take notes. That makes it easier to stay attentive, and it shows you're genuinely interested.

Dig deeper

With the *ask* part done, it's a common reflex to start talking about our own plans. Sometimes that's because we want the expert's input, but often we just want to show what we already know. My advice? Don't waste your time. Ask follow-up questions instead, to fully take in what's being said.

When you're picking someone's brain, you want to understand exactly what they mean. Keep in mind that the first answer never tells the whole story. There's always more to it. Whether you end up getting the whole story depends on the quality of your follow-up questions. Here are some suggestions to help:

- "Could you tell me a little more about that?"
- "Before we go on, could we go back to that last point? How did that go exactly?" Or: "How did that choice come about?"
- "How do you look back on that now?"
- "What would you do differently, given the chance?"

Take notes

You'll start to process what you hear during the conversation itself. So take notes. I know I always seem to remember more when I take notes, even if I never look at them again. Jotting along with the conversation also means I'm present and alert and less easily distracted, especially when doing talks by video call. (If you can't or don't want to take notes during your meeting, make sure to do it right afterward.) Interesting people always share other interesting things to explore: tips on other people to talk to, books to read, or blog posts you'll want to check out. So raid your notes for any gems and turn them into new to-dos or calendar items.

Finding good people to tell you what they know is the first step, but actually *doing* something with all that information is its own challenge. I've found that taking a moment to work through my notes right afterward gives me the momentum to act. For more pointers on note-taking, flip to the back of this book where I share my techniques (in the bonus chapter "Keeping Better Notes").

Try it out

Applying the tips and advice you get is an essential part of listening well. Whether that means trying out a new tool or deciding whether to read a recommended book, any pointers clever people give you are worth taking seriously. Make your default, "Great, I'll check that out." My mentor (more on him later) often gives me tips that can at first sound like the long and hard way of doing things, but in hindsight always turn out to be worthwhile.

Say thanks

The last step of listening isn't part of resolving your issue as such, but it will help you down the road. It's amazing how many people ask for advice and then never bother to acknowledge the favor (apart from asking to connect on LinkedIn). By that I mean a simple acknowledgment like: "Hey, thanks for taking the time to talk to me! You gave me some great tips about X and I just ordered that book you mentioned." Never assume the other person doesn't want to hear about it. Thanking someone who's taken the time to advise you shows you value them and you're putting their ideas and suggestions to use. It also opens the door to further dialogue. Showing that you're making the most of their input ups the odds they'll want to help you out again.

WHO SHOULD YOU LISTEN TO?

If you're anything like me, you've got a couple of people you turn to when you get stuck. But have you considered sounding out someone new? That can be incredibly useful, especially if you make a point of listening well. But who should you listen to? To figure out the best person to talk to in a given context, two factors are key: what they know about the topic and what they know about you and your situation.

Knowledge about the topic

Who really knows the ins and outs of whatever you're grappling with? Let's say you want to buy a house. You'll pay serious attention to tips from existing homeowners, but you'll learn a lot more by asking that friend in real estate or the acquaintance who's bought several houses before. Want really good advice? Start with people specialized in what you have questions about. That said, knowledgeable people do have one potential drawback: they can be stuck in their own mode of problem-solving.

That's why it's also a good idea to ask *why* they favor a particular solution, and what other options they *don't* recommend. If you can, get a second opinion from another expert. They might provide surprising new angles.

Knowledge about you and your situation

Someone who knows what you want, as well as your strengths and weaknesses, can be a big help. They understand you and your situation. This can be a friend, family member, your partner, or a coworker. But consulting these people has a downside. They may not be completely honest for fear of hurting you or your relationship. So bear that in mind.

Advisor matrix

Feed these two factors—knowledge about the topic and knowledge about you and your situation—into a matrix, and you end up with four different types of advisors. Let's take a look at how they can help.

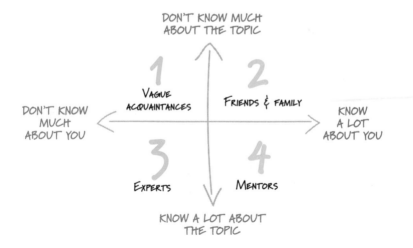

QUADRANT 1. VAGUE ACQUAINTANCES

I'll start with the least attractive category of advisors: the vague acquaintance. These are people who don't know much about you or your situation and aren't experts either, so they're unlikely to have a sound answer to your question. They may be bright or accomplished, but they lack experience in the thing you want advice about. Any information you get from a vague acquaintance needs to be verified first. That said, this type of advisor can still be useful. The fact that they're not experts makes them more likely to take a fresh angle and have creative new insights. Also look at how and why they arrive at their advice. You may learn something from their reasoning. And there's always a chance they can connect you with someone who *is* an expert.

QUADRANT 2. FRIENDS AND FAMILY

Close friends and family know you well. They can put themselves in your shoes. The fact that they know you and your situation makes them the perfect sparring partners: you present your problem, they respond. But there's also good reason to be cautious. Friends may be reluctant to be truly critical. Friends who aren't experts also won't be able to give you tried-and-tested solutions, but may not hesitate to push their own views. In spite of these drawbacks, friends can still help you find answers:

- Friends can share their insight into *you*. Which solution do they think best fits you? A couple of years ago, I was considering taking a big hiking trip abroad. To help me decide, I asked some friends if they thought I'd enjoy it. Their encouragement dispelled my doubts and I ended up having a fantastic time hiking through Austria. I still needed seasoned hikers to advise me on gear, but it was my friends who convinced me I'd love trekking through the mountains.

- Because they know you well, friends can help you dissect a problem. So, instead of turning to them for a fix, see if they can help you get a handle on what's wrong.
- Friends are happy to help you find experts.

QUADRANT 3. EXPERTS

The question here isn't, *Is there an expert?* The question is, *Who's the best expert given this situation?* That's the person you want. Much as I learn from management books and videos, a single good discussion with an expert teaches me exactly what I need to know about a topic in a fraction of the time. Here are some of my tips for making the most of talking to experts:

- **Find the right expert.** Take the time to figure out who's best equipped to help. Does this expert have practical experience with your issue? Has he or she had notable successes in this area (or failures you'd like to ask about)?
- **Schedule a meeting.** By far the best way to reach out to people you don't know is through a mutual connection. Don't have one? Second best is emailing the expert your question. And regardless of whether you have a go-between, the more straightforward your request, the more likely people will be willing to make time for you. You could try suggesting a quick half-hour meeting at their favorite coffee place. The coffee's on you, of course, and be mindful not to run over time.
- **Come prepared.** We all value our time and you're asking a favor. So come prepared. Many experts share their know-how on LinkedIn, Twitter, or their own websites; check out those

sources beforehand. If you want to get the most out of talking to an expert, have a set of concrete questions ready. If the issue's more complex, I also like to email some background info to the person in advance. Keep your reasons for the meeting in mind as you prepare.

- **Don't get defensive.** Consulting an expert tends to hold a mirror up to your own actions. When that happens, it's natural to want to defend yourself. After all, the person across from you doesn't know your specific situation and you're not doing so bad, right? But that kind of reaction won't get you anywhere. It certainly won't get you what you want to know. And it's frustrating for others when you seem to be asking for their advice, but you're really just asking for their approval. Whenever you consult an expert, remember that your job is to listen and learn.

- **Clarify your limitations.** If you know right away that you can't apply their advice because of technical, financial, or even legal reasons, fill the person in about your limitations and then ask for their input again. At Blendle, for example, we had specific agreements with newspaper and magazine publishers about how we could supply their articles. Those contracts also determined whether we could execute some of our own plans or not. If an expert suggested a solution I instantly knew wasn't doable, I gave them that extra context. Often, I got new advice that was a better fit.

- **Last but not least: enjoy the conversation!** Nothing beats talking to bright people who are willing to share their experience. This is your chance to learn from a pro.

QUADRANT 4. MENTORS

A mentor is a very different kind of advisor from an expert because a mentor is someone you talk to regularly. Besides being knowledgeable and experienced, a good mentor is also familiar with your situation. Since you're in frequent contact, you've built up a rapport. All this can make a mentor's advice spot-on and—as you grow closer—more attuned to what you need.

A mentor is someone you look up to. Preferably not a co-worker, because they have a stake in your work. Since that's not true with outside mentors, they can advise you more objectively. One thing I hear a lot is: *A mentor sounds great, but how do I find one?* Here are two tips:

1. Talk with more experts. I met my mentor through an expert—who I met in turn through another expert. I'd never have found my mentor if I hadn't pushed myself to keep meeting new people. Talking with experts is classic *important* and *non-urgent* activity of the kind we looked at in chapter 1. Good mentors don't just show up on your doorstep. So keep at it. You're looking for someone with expert-level knowledge who's able to tune in to what you need. Finding someone with just the right combination of qualities can take some time, but it's absolutely worth it.

2. Don't look for a mentor for everything, but only for a specific matter. Finding someone who can be a role model in both your work and personal life is next to impossible. You'll have much better luck finding someone who can advise you about a particular facet of your work or a specific personal issue.

My experience, and that of other people I know who have mentors, is that a mentor is somebody whose input you'd like more often. They're someone who challenges you more than others, that you feel freer to share details and uncertainties with, and who asks pointed questions and makes good suggestions. Met an expert who fits this description? Great! Give it a little time and then ask if you can talk again.

The etiquette here is the same as for a good informational meeting: come prepared, know what you want to know, and use the *Listen Better* techniques from this chapter. Did this second meeting help you out? Then go ahead and ask this expert if they'd be willing to mentor you for a longer period.

Mentorship is basically an arrangement to talk regularly. In my case, for an hour once a month. Since you're the one asking the favor, you're also responsible for the scheduling, preparation, and updates. Here's how that works:

Scheduling. Schedule your discussions well in advance at a time and place that's convenient for your mentor. My mentor lives in California, so occasionally the timing's not great for me over in Amsterdam. But that's part of the deal, because our talks are worth it.

Preparation. Your mentor makes their valuable time available to you, so to show up unprepared would be disrespectful. I like to gather everything I want to discuss in a Google Docs file we can both access. I'll update this list before our session and send my mentor an email reminder and document link. Good points for discussion include dilemmas you're grappling with and things that haven't gone as well or smoothly recently as you'd like. There's a good chance your mentor can advise you on how to head off those problems in the future.

Updates. Talking to your mentor (like other experts) should leave you with a list of ideas to try next. Be sure to update your mentor on your progress. It's great input for your next meeting, and your feedback will deepen the mentorship. By acting on the tips your mentor shares with you, and letting them know how things went, you're showing your mentor that you value their advice and want to incorporate it into your own practice. Updates don't have to be complicated—just a quick email summing up your actions and outcomes is enough.

A good mentor is worth their weight in gold. A mentor gets to know you well over time and can help you move forward faster than you ever could on your own. My mentor has guided me toward better choices—who to hire, how to plan my days, and what books to check out. And he's taught me to think more carefully about what matters to me in the long run. His input was invaluable when one of my team members and I didn't see eye to eye. Our visions were forking off in different directions and we'd had an unpleasant exchange. When I told my mentor about it, his advice was simple and spot-on: Take some time to sit down with this guy and understand the picture in *his* head. Give him a whiteboard, listen to *his* perspective. I took the advice and set up a meeting with my colleague. That marked a turning point in our relationship, because now we both understand where the other person's coming from. The experience was a real eye-opener for me. I realized my frustration had blinded me to this practical solution, and my mentor gave me exactly what I needed.

So keep reaching out—to mentor, friend, expert, acquaintance, and colleague—and listen to what people have to say. It's a surefire way to get more out of work and out of life.

10. SOLVE ANY PROBLEM
Learning to think strategically

Be honest. When's the last time you thought long and hard about something? I mean *really* racked your brain? Or how about the last time you looked back and regretted *not* giving a particular decision more thought? How many times have you been blindsided by how long something takes or how complicated it turns out to be?

In this chapter I'm going to help you raise your thinking to a higher level. And I'll give you my best tip up front: make time to think. If you can do that, you're already ahead of the game. Make room for your thoughts. Set aside *thinking time* in your calendar (because if it's in there, you'll do it). And whatever you're pondering, by all means write about it, sketch it out, and sleep on it.

MAKE THINKING A PRIORITY

Maybe you know the feeling: You're standing in the shower when suddenly you have a flash of insight. Out of nowhere you see a solution for that thing that's been bugging you for days. Those eureka moments feel fantastic. Some people call them *epiphanies*, like bolts from the blue. But that's misleading.

Usually you've been mulling over the issue for a while, whether you know it or not. The problem and possible solutions were already brewing in your head.

It's like how you see Volkswagens all over the place when you're thinking of buying one yourself. To your brain, VWs are a trending topic, so it sends you a signal whenever they pass by. That's because your brain snaps up all the tidbits of information you give it, both at a conscious and an unconscious level. And that's pretty useful. You can actually harness this brainpower by doing some of your own *preselecting*. By that I mean actively feeding your brain information about an issue and then giving yourself time to digest the data. This will automatically give you solutions that are more fully thought through.

Besides feeding my brain like this, I also use another, more active method to take my thinking to a higher level: *thinking strategically.*

STRATEGIC THINKING

Dilemmas. We all face our share. There are the issues you run into during your Friday recap ("Do I need to start on the PR plan for product X this week, before it's finalized? Or does it need more testing first?"). Or when working through your to-do list ("Is now the right time to recruit? And what's the job exactly?"). Or when looking back over the past year and making plans for the year ahead ("Is this a good time to enroll in an advanced course? And which one's best for me?").

Whenever you face a decision, you have three options: put off deciding (which is itself a decision), take the bull by the horns (and decide without delay), or do some strategic thinking. It's that last option I want to tell you about.

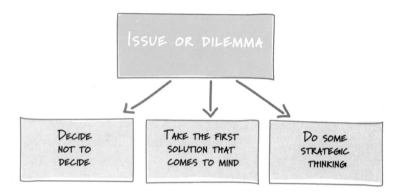

My strategic thinking approach consists of four tactics that can be used for everything from simple decisions to complex dilemmas.

The more strategically you think about a dilemma, the better the results will be. You'll organize, evaluate, plan, and work better—and who can't use that? But it only works if you take the time, so give yourself room to think.

You can use these four tactics to solve even the most perplexing problems:

1. Get to the heart of the problem
2. Look at what others have tried
3. Come up with alternatives
4. Spot your own bias (and correct for it)

I like applying the tactics in this order, but you can also pick and choose. So let's see what they can do.

Strategic thinking

| 1.
GET AT THE
CORE PROBLEM | 2.
LOOK AT EXISTING
SOLUTIONS | 3.
COME UP WITH
ALTERNATIVES | 4.
SPOT BIAS AND
CORRECT FOR IT |

In the heat of brainstorming, it's easy to be enticed by a possible way out of your dilemma. You can already picture the end result and are eager to take action. While that enthusiasm is great, it can also be a major pitfall. I've been to my share of meetings where everyone's satisfied with the outcome—until someone asks, "So have we solved it?" and we're all left scratching our heads. Turns out, the outcome wasn't everything we thought it was. Want to come up with better solutions? Then spend more time grappling with the problem. The better you understand what's wrong, the better your solution will be.

Let's say you run a restaurant and revenue is down. Without thinking much about the problem, you can come up with a number of fixes. You could launch a delivery service, expand outdoor seating, or hire a new cook. And who knows, with good instincts and a bit of luck, that might do the trick. But the bigger the shortfall and the more cash you need to throw at it, the less sense an intuitive approach makes.

What you need is to find the root cause. Here are three questions that can help you get to the heart of the problem:

Question 1. Do you understand why your problem's a problem?

Before thinking up possible causes, let alone solutions, you need to get a handle on what's actually going wrong. Is revenue the issue, or are your costs too high? What does your budget tell you? And your bank account? How big is the problem exactly? How much money do you need? Concentrating solely on the problem first—without veering off into solutions—keeps you from wasting time and money on something that fails to address the underlying issue.

Question 2. What do you think is causing the problem?

If the problem's in your court, you're probably best positioned to see the root causes. Try writing out—or drawing—an overview of what you see. Doing this makes the problem more concrete, and in a way that's easier to share with others too.

Another method I find really helpful here is the old *five whys* technique. Going back to our restaurant example, we could approach the problem like this:

- Why is revenue down? → Because the number of patrons has dropped in recent months.
- Why has the number of patrons dropped in recent months? → Because many of them booked via a particular website and those numbers have declined.
- Why has the number of bookings from that site declined? → Because of a bad review posted there.
- Why did your restaurant get a bad review? → Because the waitstaff failed to meet a patron's dietary needs and the menu was unclear.
- Why was the menu unclear? → The patron couldn't tell if dishes contained a particular ingredient.

Don't be surprised if it takes some sleuthing to get to the bottom of your five whys. In our example, you had to figure out that lots of patrons found the restaurant through this one website, read all the reviews on that site, figure out who was working that day, and so on. But once you've done this work, you'll have a pretty clear sense of the problem's root cause.

As the restaurant's owner, you can then use these answers to take targeted action, like updating the menu and offering the dissatisfied diner a free meal in hopes of getting a glowing review. Making this relatively small change—based on solid research—can make a big difference.

Sometimes it's also a good idea to look at your problem's context and history. Let's say you want to launch a new retail chain. You know that lots of major chains have folded in recent years. So what are the odds yours will succeed? To answer this, you have to spend some time digging into the background of other chains. What caused those bankruptcies? What secondary factors contributed? Were chains in all regions equally affected? Were there any that actually saw business pick up? What enabled them to survive? Getting a clear picture of the context and history of the sector can help you better understand the problem.

Question 3. Why are you losing customers or users?

Does the problem you're trying to unravel involve other people? If it's connected to customer or user behavior, there's only one way to get to the bottom of it. Talk to your customers! What problem or difficulty have they run into? Focus on what they're experiencing and how they feel about it. That's what matters.

When I worked at Blendle, it was located in an office complex at the heart of downtown. The lower floors house this massive shopping mall that feeds into the country's largest train station. It's a constant coming-and-going of people, all day long. We'd often just walk downstairs to ask folks what they thought of our work. These spontaneous polls helped us answer questions like why people weren't using some new functionality. We almost always gleaned fresh insight from the responses we got. Of course, not every office has thousands of people passing by downstairs. If you can reach folks by email, try asking them for some quick feedback that way.

In our restaurant example, polling your patrons might reveal that the problem has nothing to do with the quality or price of the food, but that your hours are inconvenient. And that's easy to fix.

CHECKLIST FOR GETTING TO THE HEART OF THE PROBLEM
- Try to define your problem in precise terms.
- Get to the root of the problem, using the five whys.
- Talk to the people affected to find out what's causing the problem.
- Redefine the problem to include this root cause.

Think you've got a handle on the problem? Then it's time to move on to our second tactic: looking at existing solutions.

2. LOOKING AT WHAT OTHERS HAVE TRIED

Strategic Thinking

| 1. GET AT THE CORE PROBLEM | 2. LOOK AT EXISTING SOLUTIONS | 3. COME UP WITH ALTERNATIVES | 4. SPOT BIAS AND CORRECT FOR IT |

Back in 2014, Blendle decided to redesign its *onboarding* experience. That's the way new users get acquainted with a digital product up through the moment they actually sign up. Because it's a customer's first—and maybe only—introduction to the product, it's a key part of acquisitions for any web-based company.

We came up with some new onboarding features we felt confident about, but in this case I really wanted to take a systematic approach. After all, developing the software was going to be a big job. So it was worth the extra effort to find out if we were on the right track or if our solution needed more work.

I took thirty days to get the lay of the land, examining a different digital product's onboarding process each day. This seemed to me like a simple approach that wouldn't take much time—and it worked great. The fieldwork took no more than half an hour a day. I noted the pros and cons of signing up for a product and posted everything on my blog.[1] And though my total time investment was limited, in a month I'd become our onboarding expert.

Armed with my new insights, I came up with ways we could hone our own approach. That led directly to several design improvements that definitely paid off. Were they revolutionary changes? Not at all. But looking at tried-and-true methods gave us a solid basis for our own onboarding features.

In chapter 9, we already saw how talking to experts can speed up your learning curve. When researching solutions, you're basically doing the same thing: taking the time to analyze how others have tackled a problem. And why *wouldn't* you take advantage of existing know-how? I mean, if you run a restaurant, you can learn a lot from visiting other eateries in the neighborhood.

Here's another example. Let's say a particular brand of shoes you want is hard to find. You see an opportunity and decide to start a webshop to sell them yourself. It's good to scope out the field and see what other vendors are doing first. But how?

- Start in the most obvious place and look at other webshops that sell shoes. You could adapt my onboarding approach: look up a different webshop every day and write down what strikes you. What do you like about their shopping experience? What makes their website inviting and accessible (or not)? Which features do you like and dislike? You could start out with webshops that are all about the same size and have a similar range of products, but can also branch out to stores that are much larger or more specialized. If you want to be super thorough, you might even order a product from each one. You're sure to pick up on details competitors haven't.
- The next step is a little less obvious. Study companies that do something similar but differ from your venture in some fundamental way. You could look at shoe webshops abroad (different place), webshops for gadgets (different sector), or brick-and-mortar shoe stores (different retail channel).
- Want to go even broader? Then expand your selection criteria to look at companies that don't sell products, but services. Or at vendors specialized in one link in your product chain, like parcel services. Or at companies that make shoes and don't just sell them.

Besides analyzing other people's ideas, it can also be incredibly useful to talk to the experts behind those ideas. Of course, insiders at direct competitors may not want to divulge their secrets. But companies and ventures operating in a different market or serving a different target group are good options to try.

CHECKLIST FOR ANALYZING OTHER PEOPLE'S SOLUTIONS

- Spend at least an hour looking at other solutions.
- Talk to one or more experts about possible solutions.
- Go deeper: study existing solutions and list their pros and cons.
- Analyze solutions in your own sector, but also across a broader cross section.

Researching what others have done before you and carefully analyzing the problem will go a long way toward getting you on the right track. By this point, chances are you've even found a solution you like. But don't make a choice just yet because the third tactic can reveal more promising alternatives.

Inventing is nothing new

To invent is to expand upon an existing idea. Take big technological revolutions. The invention of the steam engine sparked the Industrial Revolution. Put a steam engine on a wheeled cart and you've got the rudiments of the modern automobile. Put that cart on a series of metal rails and you've got a train. And the steam engine wasn't completely new either because back in the first century people had already come up with the aeolipile. This was a water-filled sphere with two projecting tubes that, when placed over a heat source, rotated from the force of the ejected steam. So taking the time to study existing ideas just might inspire your biggest breakthrough yet!

STRATEGIC THINKING

Over the years I've learned that the first solution I come up with is rarely the best. And it won't come as any surprise that mediocre solutions tend to produce mediocre results. But most of the time, we do the first thing that springs to mind. We have our brains to thank for that. Thinking takes energy (remember Kahneman's System 2, on p. 40), and our brains are hardwired for maximum efficiency.

With that in mind, I'd like to urge you to come up with more possible solutions to your dilemmas. How you do that is up to you, so the challenge is to figure out which approach helps you do your best thinking. Maybe it's carrying around a notebook to jot down ideas as they arise or—at the other extreme—sitting down for an extended session to think about one thing. My co-worker Noor has her best ideas when brainstorming with Post-its on a whiteboard, even if she's alone. What works well for me is to block time in my calendar for brainwork. Ideally, not on the day the issue needs to be fixed, but as far in advance as possible. Even better is if I can spread my thinking out over multiple blocks in a week. By assigning a problem to the whole week, I know I'll have flashes of insight outside my scheduled times for thinking, when I'm loading the dishwasher or brushing my teeth.

But what if you hit a wall and can't come up with more solutions? Odds are it's because you're rejecting every alternative as soon as it occurs to you. Try withholding judgment at this stage. Write down all your brain waves, no matter how silly they seem. Because there's a good chance that taking another look at these "rejects" will open your eyes to new possibilities.

Here are some questions to inspire more solutions:

- What would I do if I had unlimited time, money, and resources?
- What would I do if I had to solve this within the next hour?
- What would a solution that's "simple" and "intuitive" look like?
- What would my solution be if I could start over from scratch?
- Is there a solution that's even simpler?

CHECKLIST FOR COMING UP WITH ALTERNATIVES
- Don't stop until you've come up with a range of different solutions.
- Write down your options by hand, or draw them out on paper, Post-its, or a whiteboard.
- Work out the pros and cons of your solutions to crystallize your thinking.
- Give it time. Sleep on it or take a long walk.
- Talk about the problem and possible fixes with your partner in crime (chapter 7) or your mentor or an expert (chapter 9).

Having a whole bunch of solutions to choose from is great, but how do you prune them down to just one? This is where the fourth tactic comes in, which reveals where your brain is throwing you off.

4. SPOTTING YOUR OWN BIAS
(AND CORRECTING FOR IT)

Strategic thinking

Your brain is working nonstop to make sense of the world as best it can. It uses all kinds of mechanisms to do so, things that data analysts can only dream of. For starters, your brain is a master categorizer. Say I show you a picture of a random desk. You'd know instantly it was a place to work, without ever having seen that particular monitor or notebook or stapler. This is just one example of how our brains draw conclusions based on minimal data. In many cases, those snap judgments work pretty well. But in situations calling for serious brainwork, the same mechanism can mislead you without you ever knowing.

To have any hope of solving complex problems strategically, we need to recognize these mechanisms. American author and entrepreneur Buster Benson has done extensive research on *cognitive bias.*[2] He classifies it into four groups:

1. Our brains filter things

Our brains are overloaded with information, so they're constantly filtering things out: a) things that are normal to you, b) things that resemble other things, and c) things that don't square with your worldview. So, when looking to solve a problem, it's important to be extra attentive. Otherwise, your brain won't register things you consider ordinary or things you don't believe in.

2. Our brains fill in the gaps

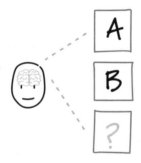

When we're missing information, our brains complete the picture using familiar patterns, generalizations, and stereotypes. What's more, our experience of the present automatically shades our view of the past and future. As a result, we tend to assume that our past actions were driven by the same values we have now.

3. Our brains prefer fast to slow

Being able to make quick decisions is essential for survival, so our brains have created some handy shortcuts for this. They prioritize things in the here and now, for instance, over things in the future.

4. Our brains remember things creatively
Our brains compress memories and fill in gaps. They twist facts and sometimes invent details of what we remember.

Completely rooting out these four types of cognitive bias is impossible, but once you know what to look for, you can get better at detecting bias. At the start of this chapter I gave you a tip:

Make time to think. Now I want to give you another: *Make time to deal with the four ways your brain misleads you.* Examining our own assumptions more closely can uncover bias. That's something we can encourage each other to do. The following questions can help shed critical light on potential solutions and choices.

THE BIG COGNITIVE BIAS CHECKLIST

Do I like this idea because:

- . . . I happened to come across it recently?
- . . . it feels familiar?
- . . . it's particularly striking or startling?
- . . . it's new, unlike other solutions?
- . . . it perfectly matches my worldview?
- . . . it's my idea (and other people's ideas are never as good)?
- . . . I'm seeing a pattern that may not really be there?
- . . . it fits with a stereotype or generalization that feels right?
- . . . someone I like thought of it?
- . . . someone I don't like thought of the other solutions?
- . . . it's nice and simple?
- . . . the other solution is so hard to get my head around?
- . . . I think I know how others think?
- . . . I think I know how it will turn out?
- . . . I've linked it to a picture of the past that I'm 100 percent certain about?
- . . . I just know it's a sure thing?
- . . . I'm optimistic about this idea and not about the others?
- . . . I've already started on it?
- . . . I've talked to one person who thought it was brilliant (even though there's no data to prove it yet)?

- . . . the other solutions feel too risky because they're irreversible (so I won't even look into them)?
- . . . the solution might affect my status?
- . . . I currently have the most information about it?
- . . . I had a super positive experience with it (but because brains remember creatively, that may be skewed)?
- . . . the other solutions remind me of a very negative experience?
- . . . it squares perfectly with my life experience up to now?
- . . . I've been in this exact same situation before (but was it truly the same)?

CHECKLIST FOR SPOTTING YOUR OWN BIAS AND CORRECTING FOR IT

- Be mindful that you're continually making assumptions under the influence of cognitive bias.
- Study all possible solutions and data carefully and give yourself time to decide. That will already cancel out a large part of your cognitive bias. (*Our brains filter things.*)
- Look critically at the available data. Is it complete? What do your source documents tell you? By taking a rational view, you can keep from making decisions based on incorrect information. (*Our brains fill in the gaps.*)
- Are you leaning toward a solution because of the short-term rewards? Check that you're also considering its impacts over the longer term. (*Our brains prefer fast over slow.*)
- If you remember a solution worked for you in the past, double-check if the memory's accurate. Do you have data to back that up? Protect yourself from falling into the trap of a creative memory. (*Our brains remember things creatively.*)

Finding a selection of good solutions to big and complex challenges isn't easy. Having thought through the problem, lined up and compared a variety of solutions, and taken steps to guard against cognitive bias, the last step is to choose. But before you make that final decision, there are two more things you can do to take your thinking to a higher level.

1. BE MORE CRITICAL OF YOUR OWN IDEAS

No matter how enthusiastic everyone else is about your idea, it's important to stay critical. That might sound like a contradiction to what I wrote earlier—to gather better solutions by thinking up more of them—but in the end you can *do* only one. So it's essential to be able to critique your own ideas, especially when there's a lot at stake, like the future of your company, or choosing a degree, or deciding whether to take a job. Time then to trade those rose-tinted glasses for a magnifying glass and reexamine your own and other people's assumptions. Question *everything*.

Here are some pointers for taking a critical look at your own ideas:

- Remember that there's always another angle to whatever you're trying to solve. Take vaccination. Injecting a tiny dose of disease to *prevent* that same disease doesn't sound like the most obvious fix. But some vaccines do just that, and it's made the world a much healthier place.
- Ask yourself: *What would a 100 percent rational version of me do?* This question can help you detect differences between your emotional and your rational self.

- Respect your intuition. If your gut feeling is to reject an idea, it could be good to dig a little deeper. Is there more data to explore?
- Ask yourself: *What would [insert your hero] do?*
- Test the facts. For instance: "We need to do plan A, because it will boost earnings at least 40 percent more than plan B." Here, it makes sense to verify whether this percentage checks out.
- Articulate assumptions. We all have them, and it's good to get them out in the open. To think critically, it's vital to recognize when you're dealing with assumptions—and then test them.
- Also look at what's *not* being said. Sometimes there are good reasons for it, sometimes not, but either way you can learn a lot from gaps. Let's say you're screening job applicants. A useful question could be: Which quality is *not* mentioned in this person's cover letter or resume? Asking *What's missing here?* helps you see the situation from a new angle.

2. DOCUMENT YOUR DECISIONS

The only way we can ever know if a solution is any good is to carry it out and watch what happens. The proof of the pudding is in the eating. That means we need to document our solutions and look back on them later with some distance, after some time has passed or the project's done. This documentation doesn't need to be complicated. I keep a digital *Decisions* notebook to remind me of all my important decisions. I write down what I decided and when, in the simplest form possible, usually a single sentence: "Decided on [date] to hire candidate A" or "Decided on [date] to stop Project X." If you want, you can also add the rationale for your decision and any alternatives you rejected.

In this chapter we saw how strategic thinking results in much better decisions—whatever the issue or dilemma. When you stop to think about it, it's weird we don't learn these techniques earlier and then use them every chance we get.

11. THINK BIG
And start small

Thinking big takes you further than you'd think. In chapter 10, I mentioned my project at Blendle where I looked at a new onboarding experience every day for thirty days. The story didn't end there.

By the end of that month I knew I'd harvested some really useful information. While cycling home one day, I had a stroke of inspiration: Why not turn what I'd learned into an article and try submitting it to one of my favorite websites? I emailed the editors at *A List Apart,* a respected online magazine in the web-development world. After all, nothing ventured, nothing gained. Just *asking* them to publish my piece felt like clearing a high hurdle. Amazingly, they liked the idea. So was my draft article good to go? Well, no. Not even close. By the time it went online, just a few snippets of the original text were left. Only after weeks of reworking and polishing my piece under the meticulous eye of a brilliant editor at *A List Apart* was it ready to post.[1]

After publication, I got dozens of enthusiastic reactions from developers around the world. And that's not all. What had started out as a simple thirty-day blog project led to all sorts of unexpected things. A couple of months later, I found myself on a stage in Oslo talking about onboarding to an auditorium packed with Norwegians.[2]

Even this book grew out of that onboarding adventure. After thirty days of blogposting, I had a newfound appetite for writing and decided to start my own daily newsletter. Every day over the next year I shared my ideas with a growing readership about developing better online products and smarter ways to work. Soon, people were encouraging me to do more with all that material. Like write a book. And so, chapter by chapter, I did. Though not much from the original posts made it in, the book steadily grew. The result is what's before you now.

Personal triumphs are the sum of a long chain of tiny acts. And I'm not talking rocket science here. I mean things like appointments in your calendar, an email here, a to-do there. Regular sessions with your partner in crime and your Friday recap. If you can set doable goals and work toward them one step at a time, you'll be amazed at what you can accomplish.

So now let's crank things up a notch. Time to think big. Thinking big (1) helps you come up with the next step to take (2). Taking that step gives you a new perspective on what's possible (3), which helps you think bigger still, putting you on the way to another next step.

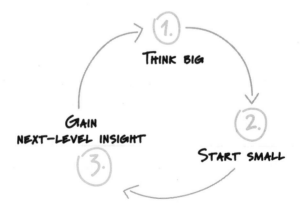

Boyan Slat is a young Dutch inventor. His startup The Ocean Cleanup wants to get rid of the vast quantity of plastic polluting the world's oceans. Slat was gripped by this problem ever since writing a paper about it in high school. While he could have chosen any number of things to focus on, he's decided to devote himself day in, day out, to this huge challenge.

What I especially like is the way he does this: Slat and his team keep trying out all kinds of different solutions. If an idea isn't working, he's willing to completely shift his approach. While it's easy to dismiss his ideas or criticize what doesn't work, he's actively chasing a clear goal and getting concrete results. And that means raising awareness and gaining greater insight into this important issue.

Or take Malala Yousafzai, who earned worldwide fame by blogging for the BBC at age eleven (under a pseudonym) about the violence of the Taliban regime. Undeterred even by an attempt on her life, she continues to advocate for human rights and schooling for girls.

Then there's Mette Lykke, who launched the startup Too Good To Go with a mission to stop food waste. She created an app that supermarkets, bakeries, and eateries can use to offer their leftover food products to consumers rather than just throwing them away.

No less inspiring is a campaign launched by Johnas van Lammeren, member of the Amsterdam city council, to tamp down on paper waste. We already have legislation in the Netherlands that allows households to opt out of getting advertising flyers in the mail. You just add a sticker to your mailbox, which basically says *No thanks*. But van Lammeren managed to reverse this rule for Amsterdam. Now you have to *opt in*. People who want advertising circulars delivered to their door must actively say so. His efforts save more than 11,000 tons of paper each year.

These are all examples where one individual is working to try to make the world a better place. And while people might call them crazy, that doesn't knock down their ambitions.

I want to challenge you to give this a try too. Up your ambitions, for whatever you want. Plan that trip around the world. Start that business you always wanted. Throw yourself into solving that giant global problem. Or organize to help your community. Make a change to a new job or a new field. Move to a new city or country. Yes, going for a big goal will require loads of time and energy. And it won't be easy—if it were, everyone would do it. But this is where you can make a difference. So think big and begin.

A LONG VIEW BRINGS PEACE OF MIND

Making big plans takes time. And that's exactly why we tend to avoid them: we like our results fast. But that's a shame because we generally have more time than we think. I'm willing to bet you have the time to pursue a goal for ten, twenty, or even fifty years. Just imagine what you could achieve in that time. Bill Gates put it like this: "Most people overestimate what they can do in one year and underestimate what they can do in ten."

Taking a long view also gives you more room to breathe. *Especially* at times in life when you're under massive pressure to perform. You want to make things happen now—this year, this month, or better yet, TODAY. Extending your perspective offers a counterweight to this pressure. Not everything needs to be done right now. You can also work on a more distant outcome one step at a time. It's even worth asking what's more satisfying:

Doing your best work before you turn thirty? Or when you hit seventy-five?

In his book *The Clock of the Long Now*, Stewart Brand gives some pointers for looking even further. Brand and his organization built a clock that ticks once a year. It won't chime for ten thousand years.[3] Talk about a long view! Brand stresses that "there are problems that are impossible if you think about them in two-year terms—which everyone does—but they're easy if you think in fifty-year terms."

If we really want to make a difference and contribute something meaningful, then we have to break out of our preoccupation with today, this week, this year, and maybe even our own lifetimes, and start thinking about the grand scheme of things. Then the question isn't *whether* you can do something, but *what* it is you're going to do.

BACK TO YOUR CALENDAR

Whatever your ambition, starting out with your calendar and the week's priorities can help you do what you aspire to do. I'm convinced that with the basics covered, we can accomplish great things. Only then do we have the bandwidth to think about the big stuff. And, after all, even the biggest, most ambitious tasks, when you take them apart, are just a series of little ones. They're work like any other.

You now have everything you need to take familiar tools and shape your workweek and your life in new ways. So you can get things done and get around to what matters most. And once you get the small stuff sorted, you can start thinking big. Bigger than ever before.

There's no better time to begin.

SAVE THE DATE

Want to get the most out of this book? Then mark your calendar to flip through it again six months from now. You're sure to discover new insights you can use.

NEED A HAND?

Sign up for handy reminders at gripbook .com/app and I'll help you apply the methods in this book to your workweek. You'll get a message from me when it's time for weekly and yearly recaps.

MORE TIPS?

Sign up for my newsletter at gripbook.com and get a new tip to try each week. *Work in Progress* helps you get a handle on work and get around to what matters most—one week at a time.

CHEAT SHEET
FOR PART 3

Listening well (p. 193)

- Get a clear picture of your issue or dilemma and consult experts.
- Write out your questions beforehand.
- Don't be too easily satisfied with the answers: ask good follow-ups.
- Take notes during your conversation and go through them afterward.
- Apply what you hear. When you talk to bright people, take their tips seriously.
- Report back on your experiences to the person who advised you.

Solving problems (p. 207)

- Do you have a solid grasp of the problem?
- Have you looked at existing solutions?
- Have you come up with alternatives?
- Did you work to spot your own bias and correct it?

BONUS CHAPTER:
KEEPING BETTER NOTES

Using an app to jot down your thoughts (and find them again)

Taking notes is smart. For starters, you absorb more of what you hear. Without notes, there's no way to remember all the ground covered in meetings and what was decided. Good ideas all too easily evaporate if you don't jot them down somewhere.

When it comes to notes, I like having a bigger canvas to work with than that little task field of my digital to-do list (p. 44). In chapter 2, I urged you to stop saving things in your head. And that goes for the outcomes of discussions and your own ideas too. Those belong in a digital note-taking app. Which one you pick is up to you. Most of the pointers I'll give you here will work with any app you'd like.

Keeping notes digitally is a deliberate choice. Because, sure, jotting stuff down on a pad of paper is super easy. Fishing it out again when you need it? Anything but.

My reasons for using a note-taking app are:

- Unlike a paper notebook, an app is easy to search.
- I have my note-taking app installed on my phone, tablet, and laptop, letting me consult my notes wherever, whenever.
- A notes app is never full, won't get lost, and gives you endless space plus all kinds of smart tools no paper notebook can

match. A good app makes it easy to capture pictures, links, tables, even handwritten memos.

- It's a place to park your thoughts for a while, so you have them down but they're not in your way.
- Some note-taking apps, like Evernote, can be linked with other apps. That makes your notes app the go-to spot for all your thoughts and ideas. Link up Instapaper, for example (an app that lets you save articles for later), and any text you highlight there is automatically clipped to Evernote.
- Most note-taking apps allow you to share notes with other people, even if they're not using the same app. Some, like Notion, make it easy to collaborate on notes.

Which app's the one for you?

There are hundreds of note-taking apps out there, all with their own pros and cons. Some other good ones to check out are the beautifully designed Notion (notion.so) and Microsoft's OneNote. Apple also has its own built-in notes app that gets rave reviews. The app landscape is changing all the time, so for an updated overview of my top suggestions, check gripbook.com/apps.

There are two basic ways you can use a note-taking app:

1. As a dropbox for your notes
2. As an organized directory for your notes

We tend to want the second system, but that takes more self-discipline. So let's start with the first, because setting up a dropbox for all your notes is a quick and massive win. And since it's more basic, a dropbox is easier to use.

1. A DROPBOX

Keeping your notes in a secure place helps you do better work. Once you know you won't lose them *and* you start going through them every now and then (more on that later), you'll feel good about taking notes in meetings, brainstorming sessions, appointments—wherever.

Using a note-taking app as a simple dropbox for your notes is a little like my approach to email (in chapter 3). Some apps come with a ready-made notebook called *Inbox*. If yours doesn't have one already, make one. This is where you create new notes. To jog your memory later, give those new notes meaningful titles. If you prefer writing notes on paper, consider trying an app that allows digital handwritten notes. Evernote, for instance, lets you jot down notes directly in the app using an Apple Pencil.

When you finish with a note, you can archive it by dragging it from your *Inbox* to your *Archive*. Better yet, delete it. Because why hold onto notes you'll never look at again?

Want to be sure you'll revisit the notes you take? No problem. Just build it into your week. Make *Review the notes in my Inbox* part of your weekly routine (chapter 4). Even though I already work in my notes Inbox all the time to do things like finalize meeting outcomes, I like the peace of mind that comes from knowing I'll see those notes again during my Friday recap. That means I run through my notes every Friday and decide if each one needs follow-up or can be deleted.

I also often use my notes app to save snippets of ideas that aren't true tasks yet. Though I could add them to my to-do list, I like the extra space this approach gives me to freely note down brain waves.

To give you an idea, here are some notes from my Inbox, from my time at the startup:

- *Prep for Data Protection Officer meeting*—This is a running list of points to discuss with the person who helps Blendle stay compliant with new privacy laws.
- *Blendle Audio ideas*—Here I've noted a couple of ideas about next steps for Blendle's text-to-speech functionality.
- *Personal Q3 goals*—I'm working on coming up with goals for next quarter and created this note to jot down ideas as they occur to me.
- *Team thoughts*—This note contains some thoughts about my team's performance and how we can make it even better.
- *Outsource*—This is a list of work and personal stuff I'd like to outsource or delegate to free up time for stuff that's more important to me.

As you can see, my notes contain a mix of things I'll need to attend to at some point. As part of my Friday recap, I go through the Inbox and decide on concrete next steps:

- Next step for *Personal Q3 goals*: Block one hour in my calendar to finalize my personal goals.
- Next step for *Audio ideas*: Add an action to my to-do list to "Go through and share audio ideas."
- Next step for *Team thoughts*: Schedule a meeting with a team member to hash out ideas for a smarter way to structure our week.

I don't archive all my notes during my Friday recap. There's always some I want to think about a bit longer without worrying about next steps yet. Those I skip over. But by going through them all one by one, I know I haven't overlooked anything urgent and that I'll see them all again next week.

In its most compact form, a notes app is no more than an Inbox and an Archive. It gives you a scratchpad for longer-running ideas and makes it easy to retrieve whatever you need. But if you want to unlock note-taking's full potential, we can take things a step further.

2. AN ORGANIZED DIRECTORY

Keeping notes not only lets you make better choices now; it can benefit you in the long run too. As a next step, group your notes into collections you're going to use later. Consider collections like books to read, new series to check out, and places to visit, like cafés, restaurants, and museums. If you're smart about organizing your notes, in time you'll build a valuable collection to dip into when the need arises. You could leverage the search function of your notes app, but searching isn't always the best answer. Instead, try grouping notes. If you group all your notes on, say, movies you want to see, you can pull up an instant to-watch list.

In short, if you want to use your notes to store ideas in a more structured way and find them when you need them, grouping your notes in digital notebooks is the way to go.

Most apps won't force you into any particular way of organizing. That freedom means the possibilities are endless, but it also means you run the risk that your stacks of notes will turn into jumbled heaps. If that happens, you may feel tempted to throw up your hands and ditch the whole thing. Remember: the more complicated the system, the harder it is to keep it up. If you feel things are getting unwieldy, it's better to stick with a dropbox. Keeping all your notes in one place is by far the biggest win.

That said, if you're ready for a more organized directory, here are some suggestions for basic notebooks alongside your Inbox and Archive:

- Work and personal—The fewer notebooks you have, the easier you make things for yourself. So, before you create all kinds of detailed sections, try working with broad categories like *work* and *personal.* You can expand later if you need more.
- Ideas—This is a notebook for ideas. If you have a "Someday" list or project in your to-do app, there's sure to be some overlap here. But when I want to start fleshing out my ideas, I like the freedom a note-taking app gives me.
- Meetings (or notebooks for recurring meetings)—It can be useful to hold onto meeting minutes and notes from other discussions. I did that for a while, but stopped when I realized I never bothered to revisit them. Now I just use my notes to create new actions and then delete the note itself. But you may find this a handy collection to have.

Beyond these basic collections, I also have specific notebooks in Evernote that are so useful to me I want to share them with you:

- Feedback—This notebook is for feedback I get, at work or anywhere else. It's a valuable collection that helps me track my own progress.

- Decisions—This is a place to record my bigger and more momentous decisions to look back on later and see if I made the right call.
- Checklists—This one's for all kinds of checklists, mostly for trips. Right now it's filled with lists of baby things we need to pack whenever we go anywhere.
- Failures—This is where I keep track of my mistakes and failures. It sounds like an awful collection, and of course in a way it is. At the same time it's a gentle way to learn from my mistakes and put things in perspective. Things that felt like massive missteps at the time tend to be irrelevant six months later.

Two last general tips for using your notes app:

1. **Keep it simple**, especially when you're just getting started. The fewer notebooks, the better. Once you've mastered the ins and outs of keeping notes, you can consider adding more notebooks.
2. **Refresh your system** every now and then. As I mentioned earlier, it's a good idea to tidy up your Inbox on a weekly basis. But I also find it helps to look critically at how I've organized my notes every couple of months or so. That way I can see what's working and what's not. It gives you a better overview and keeps the experience fresh. After I make those kinds of changes, I'm always as energized using the "new" app as when I first started.

BONUS CHAPTER:
GRIP ON VACATION
How to take off and come back with a clear head

You're back at work after a much-deserved break, feeling recharged and ready to go. And that's when it happens. You open your calendar for the day to find you're already a half-hour late for your first conference call. A glance at your mailbox shows 352 new messages. There's a stack of mail on your desk, your schedule's packed with back-to-back appointments, and you've already got a client on hold. Over lunch—a quick sandwich at your desk—you start wishing you'd never taken that trip at all.

Your frustration is all too common. That first week back from vacation can be the most stressful week of the year.

The good news is there's a smarter way of doing things, and it's not hard. All you have to do is schedule a few select moments to complete your GRIP checklists. Ready? Here they come.

1. AS SOON AS YOU KNOW YOU'RE GOING ON VACATION

You can get started on this checklist as soon as you know your vacation dates:

Put your vacation on your calendar. Though I'm generally not a fan of doing anything twice, I'm more than happy to add vacations to multiple calendars just to avoid misunderstandings.

If you're an employee, follow your employer's procedure for taking time off. Do you need permission from your boss? To arrange a replacement while you're gone? Or to log your absence on the company intranet? Many organizations have shared calendars where everyone can mark their days off.

Tell the people you work with. The earlier they know the exact dates you'll be gone, the easier it is for everyone to plan around that. I let people know by email when I'll be out so there's less risk of date mix-ups.

And my Magic Tip: Clear your calendar for the first two workdays after you get back. Do this now and you'll have enough time to regroup once you're back. (Maybe you can't cancel every single appointment, but try to keep big chunks of time free.) That's your time to get back up to speed. It may sound like overkill now, but I promise it will pay off later.

2. ONE FULL WEEK BEFORE YOU LEAVE

The last workweek before a vacation can get pretty hectic. And yet you often get an amazing amount done. You can harness this surge of pre-trip energy by making a smart plan for that week before you head off. This plan consists of your Friday recap (chapter 4) and this checklist:

Remind colleagues about your vacation. Email's fine, and so is the weekly huddle or stand-up on Monday. Don't assume anyone's checked the calendar and knows you're off after Wednesday.

Let key clients or customers know you'll be gone. Nothing's as frustrating for them as finding out you're away once you're already on the road or at the beach. Because no matter how well you arrange for your absence, a client who's in a fix may call up anyway. Of course, you can't plan for all contingencies, but telling clients about your trip ahead of time certainly helps. Now they can decide if they need anything from you *before* you take off.

Set aside some time for unexpected business at work. Clear your schedule now for that last workday before you leave, or at least for that afternoon. This buffer gives you time to respond to last-minute questions from coworkers and clients and to tie up any loose ends—so you won't still be typing emails at the gate.

Make a list of absolute must-dos for the week before you leave. What do you need to get done to leave clearheaded and worry-free? You can start by scanning your to-do list and your email, but also look through your ongoing projects and goals. Is there anything that can't wait? Try to be critical and to limit yourself to essentials. Step two is to block time for these must-dos in your calendar for the week. (In chapter 1, I show you how to set up a smart calendar.) And talk to your manager about what needs to be squared away before you go.

If you'll be gone for more than a week or so, go ahead and park all postvacation work in your to-do list. Normally I advise planning out your next workweek in your calendar, but with vacations longer than one week, I've discovered there's no point. So much will change by the time you're back that you'll have to adapt your plans anyway. A postvacation to-do list solves this problem. It keeps track of what you'll need to tackle so you don't lose sight of anything important. But to-do items give you the flexibility to reassess each task with fresh eyes before devoting any time to them.

- Pinpoint those areas where you need someone to cover for you while you're gone. Especially if you'll be away for a longer period. These may be projects you'll have to assign to someone else, meetings that need a chair, or clients who may want progress updates. Figure out who can stand in for you and then schedule time to fill them in on your duties.

If your calendar's anything like mine, you probably don't have time to take care of all this last-minute business alongside your existing commitments. But that's the whole point of this exercise: to figure out what's doable. The next step is scrapping what's not. Which meetings can you skip that last week or reschedule for when you're back? Which tasks can you delegate or put off? The key is to be honest with yourself and everyone else so you can take off with a clear head and a clean slate.

3. YOUR LAST WORKDAY BEFORE VACATION

Today is your chance to tie up loose ends. Assuming you cleared your schedule, you can now dive right in.

- Run through the must-dos you wrote down last week. Are they all done? In an ideal world, you tackled them all as planned, but the real world rarely works that way. Things come up and schedules change. First of all, don't panic. Now, assess what you can still get done today. Try to be realistic. Next: communicate. Be clear about your progress and any work that's not done. Sure, it feels frustrating to leave things unfinished, but not communicating about it is worse for everyone.

- Check your to-do list and your email. Over the past week you're sure to have added new tasks and received new emails, so take another quick look. Is there anything that absolutely can't wait? If you don't have enough time, then my advice is—you guessed it—communicate! Promise a speedy reply once you get back, but give yourself a buffer. For example: "I'll be back in the office starting August 26, so I'll get back to you later that week."

- Check with your manager and team for loose ends. You may wind up with more tasks on your plate but, again, that's why you don't have anything else planned today. Decide which actions you can get done now, delegate what you can, and communicate the results.

- Have you actually handed off everything that needed handing off?

- Double-check your calendar: Is your vacation period free of appointments and is it clear you'll be away?

- Create an automatic out-of-office reply for your email. These work best if you include the date you'll be back at work and contact information for a coworker people can get in touch with if need be. Also, be concrete. "I'll have limited access to my email" is vague and confusing, while "I won't be reading my email again until August 29" leaves no room for mix-ups.

- Another great practice is to keep your out-of-office reply in place during your first day back at work. That extra breathing room is sure to come in handy.

That's it! Work's sorted. Time to enjoy your vacation.

If you cleared your calendar (my Magic Tip from checklist 1), then you have plenty of time today and tomorrow to find out how your projects are going. These two days are all about getting back up to speed so you can make the best choices about what to focus on the rest of the week.

Action plan for catching up:

- Double-check your calendar. Just to be sure no one's called a meeting you need to attend or made plans for you today or tomorrow. If so, try to reschedule.

- For these first two days, put yourself in listening mode. Listen to what has and hasn't happened in your absence. There are sure to be things you would have done differently or need to think over. But before springing into action, get the whole story. Until you've talked to everyone or read up on things, you don't have the full context.

- Go through your email. Normally, I don't advise starting out with email, but if you've been out of the office for a while your inbox is the best place to get a handle on your work. Doing this first also stops you from tackling or resuming tasks that may have been done or become irrelevant in your absence. That's also why it's better to work from new emails to old. Just stick to the steps from chapter 3: Carefully read through each message in your inbox, decide what action's needed on your part, and add the work to your to-do list or calendar. If it's something you can get done in two minutes or less, take care of it on the spot.

- Ask colleagues for project updates based on what you've gleaned from emails and other sources.

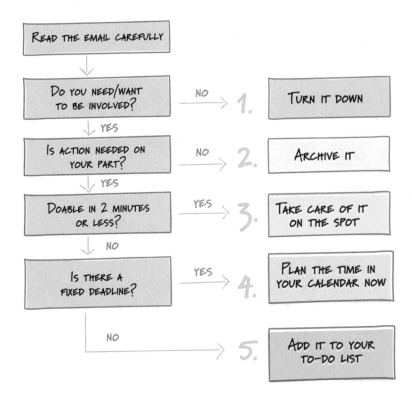

At the end of your first workday back, do a Friday recap-lite. There's a good chance you'll need to shuffle your schedule based on all this new info, so now's the perfect time to prioritize for the rest of the week.

Follow these four steps, and you're sure to take off with a clear head and dive back into your work with ease.

NEED A HAND?

Sign up for the vacation assistant that goes with this chapter. You'll get a series of timely email reminders to guide you through your trip prep, for a carefree break. You can find it here: gripbook.com/vacation.

Checklist: from chaos to calm

What happens if you can't clear your schedule for those first two days back at work? Or what if you can, but you come back to total chaos? Here's how to beat stress and get things back on track:

- If there's too much coming at you, the best thing you can do is start by giving yourself more room. See what you can cancel or postpone today. There's no point attending a meeting if you're too stressed to think straight, so call it off if you can.
- Write down what's triggering the stress and making everyone panic. Make a quick list—digitally or on paper—of everything you need to get done. What's important is getting an overview. And don't worry about the time this step takes. Because I promise this list will help.
- For every pressing issue: What will curb the stress? Is there an imminent deadline you overlooked? Then itemize what's needed to finish on time.
- Now that you've listed what needs to get done, you can judge which actions are most urgent. Put them in your calendar in order of urgency, so you can tackle the most urgent (and most stressful) task first. That brings instant relief.

- But before throwing yourself into your top task: communicate! Let's say you have three actions and want to finish two today and the third tomorrow morning. You can probably make a good estimate of when you'll deliver, so let waiting clients and colleagues know your plan.

The biggest pitfall when under pressure is trying to squash stress while still doing all your regular work. That's the opposite of efficient. By completing this checklist and giving yourself room to maneuver, you'll soon be back on top of things.

TIPS FOR DIEHARDS

- After long trips, I've discovered I go back to work more relaxed if I get home on Friday rather than Sunday evening. Restarting on Monday morning is less of a rude awakening if I've had the weekend to settle in. Some people plan vacations from Wednesday to Wednesday for the same reason. It gives you two low-key workdays to ease back into things before powering ahead again on Monday.
- If you want to go hardcore, tell people—and write in your out-of-office reply—that you won't be wading through emails that come in during your vacation. Ask them to *email you again* once you're back. That forces the senders to decide if their message will still be relevant, so you won't have to.
- The average out-of-office reply is pretty dry. Make it personal by sharing interesting blog posts, books, or even job openings.
- If you're eager to dive back in, you could try catching up on your emails on the way home. Doing so always helps me feel back in the loop. Plus it kills time on a long train trip or plane

ride. Most email programs, including Gmail, support offline use. Just open your inbox before you leave to load new messages. Then you can go through all your emails en route. As soon as you reconnect, the program will synchronize—and you'll be one step ahead.[1]

BONUS CHAPTER:
GRIP AND MANAGING A TEAM

Keeping an eye on the big picture
when you're in charge

Countless books have been written on how to become a better leader. Many delve deep into strategies of leadership and management. But the big questions for any manager are really pretty basic: What concrete things do you need to do? How do you combine all those responsibilities? And how do you keep an eye on the big picture amid all the demands of the day-to-day?

In this book I've shown you how to give direction to your work and your life. I've walked you through ways to make the most of your calendar, to-do list, and email—so you can get more done with less stress. But there's one topic I haven't covered: How do you lead a group of people? And that's intentional. Because I wanted to write a book that's relevant for everyone, not just the people in charge.

In this bonus chapter I want to share the lessons I've learned on the job over the years—first as a newly minted manager, later as a manager of managers.

You'll see me use terms like *manager, team leader,* and *supervisor* interchangeably in this chapter. While I realize there are differences, these roles have one thing in common. Not only are you responsible for your own work, but you have the privilege of working with other people to accomplish your mission. And I don't use the term *privilege* lightly. It's good to realize that we can't pull off big feats alone. While there are certainly strides you can make on your own by working smarter, there comes a point when new efficiency gains make only a marginal difference. That's when the art of working smart turns into the art of building a team.

WHAT ARE THE GOALS OF A MANAGER?

It's essential you first have a clear sense of your managerial duties. That generally comes down to two things:

1. You're responsible for the quality of products or services your organization delivers
2. You're responsible for reaching goals your organizations sets

So the manager is in charge of making the work happen, and in many cases, making it *better* than before. This could mean improving the results of a product or service, or ramping up production, or doing the same work at lower cost. If the quality of the work isn't up to par, it's usually a manager who has to answer for it. And if managers don't reach their goals, it impacts the whole organization.

Asking some basic questions lets us flesh out these two responsibilities:

- What products or services are you in charge of?
- What specifically is meant by "quality of products or services"?
- What are the organization's goals?

- Which of those goals fall under your managerial responsibility?

In my experience, most misunderstandings between different layers of management stem from conflicting answers to these questions. Say you disagree about the quality standard of your service or product. Odds are your priorities don't align with what your boss wants. To remedy the situation—or better yet, to avoid getting into it in the first place—try formulating your own answers to these four questions and then compare notes with your supervisor. Then you'll know you're on the same wavelength.

Formulating clear answers to these questions puts you miles ahead of most managers and team leaders. And once you structure your workweek to pursue your organization's products, services, and goals as a team, that's when the real magic happens. So let's talk about *how* to pursue those products, services, and goals—starting with the 3P Model.

The 3P Model

To do quality work and achieve your goals, you have three types of resources at your disposal:

1. People—Who does the work?
2. Processes—How does it get done?
3. Products—What's created?

The 3P Model is a common way of looking at organizations. Your job as a manager is to come to grips with all three elements. Here's how.

Congratulations! As a manager you're in the privileged position of not having to do everything alone. You have a team to take work off your hands. In the last few years I've noticed that two ingredients are vital when directing a team:

1. One-on-one sessions, and
2. Structural feedback.

1. One-on-ones

It was from the podcast *Manager Tools* and Andy Grove's brilliant book *High Output Management* that I first learned about one-on-ones, 1:1s, coaching sessions, check-ins, or whatever you want to call them. You can make these sessions as complicated as you like, but the essence is simple: holding thirty-minute meetings with each team member every single week. Keeping track of how your team members are doing can be tough with all the other work vying for your attention. One-on-ones let you take a moment each week to pause, take stock together, and reconnect. Every manager has their own style, and there are no rules other than making time to hear how each team member is doing.

Now, you might be thinking, *Wait a minute. Half an hour a week for every team member? Then I can kiss my whole week goodbye!* And I'm not going to argue—it is a big chunk of time. But it's also completely worth it. Not only will weekly one-on-ones save you in the long run from losing touch with your team, there are more immediate benefits too. How's it sound to no longer be peppered with one-off questions and requests all day because your staff will save them up for their next one-on-one?

Here are a few practical tips:

- **Cluster your one-on-ones.** I try to plan mine back to back on Wednesdays. It takes a lot of energy, but then you're also done for the week.
- **Keep running notes.** I keep separate notes for each team member in my notes app, adding a few comments after each meeting.
- **Use tags in your to-do list.** In chapter 2, I walked you through setting up a to-do list so there's no need to save things in your head. I also add labels for the individuals involved in tasks. That lets me filter and see at a glance what I want to discuss during this session.
- **Prioritize one-on-ones.** Try to keep these meetings going every week, come what may. Not only will you always have things to discuss, but nothing signals more clearly that your team's not important than constantly rescheduling or canceling their one-on-ones.

How big is your team?

You don't always have a say in the size of your team, and numbers can vary widely, but I find a maximum of eight direct reports seems to be ideal. Jeff Bezos, who founded Amazon, introduced the *Two-Pizza Rule*: it should be possible to feed a team with just two pizzas. Apart from the fact that bigger teams don't work as well, it's difficult for managers to give so many people good and attentive guidance. With eight, you can get through your one-on-ones in a single afternoon.

If you do lead a larger group, you could schedule one-on-ones every other week. It's not the same as connecting with your people every week, but better than leaving it to chance encounters at the watercooler.

2. Structural feedback

At Blendle, we invested a lot of time and energy in an effective feedback model. (If you're interested, the old employee handbook is available online.)[2] We felt feedback was key, and we all worked hard to build a culture where sharing positive feedback and constructive criticism with one another was the norm. We welcomed ad hoc feedback as things came up. And we set aside two fixed times a year to give and get more structural feedback, which works like this:

- All team members write a self-assessment, giving themselves a score from 1 to 5 on *impact* (What did I contribute to the organization?) and *progress* (How did I progress?), and answering three questions: 1. What are my biggest contributions to Blendle? 2. What went well? 3. What could I do better?
- Team leaders write a review for each team member.
- Everyone picks two or three coworkers (from any team) and asks for feedback, using the same form.
- Once those are submitted, team members get to see the feedback from their coworkers and team leader.
- Team leaders schedule a feedback session with each individual team member. These structural feedback meetings are expressly not performance reviews. There are no contractual consequences and they're not tied to promotions or raises. That's intentional, because you want everyone to feel free to be completely open and honest in their feedback.
- The idea is that the feedback recipient takes the wheel in these meetings. Since they're there to learn, it makes sense that they kick off the dialogue. The aim is threefold: to interpret the feedback, try to connect the dots, and chart paths for growth.

- After the meetings, team members use the feedback they got to set personal goals for the next quarter. Team leaders guide this process and help each member reach their goals.

Feedback at set times? Or anytime?

I'm a fan of periodic feedback sessions. But some people prefer foregoing those fixed meetings and sharing their feedback on an ongoing basis instead. In theory, this seems like a great idea: no more preparation, scheduling hassles, or awkward discussions. Sounds appealing! But in my experience, the practice of giving good feedback winds up fading to the background. There's no way around it—giving good, thoughtful feedback simply takes time and energy.

Here's what helps me write reviews that my people actually get something out of:

- **Keep structured notes about team members.** Try to get into the habit of noting down specific observations (the good and the bad) somewhere. Again, I keep notes about each member of my team in a note-taking app. That makes a big difference when it's time to write reviews.
- **Plan time for review-writing well in advance.** Writing reviews is a big job, and not having enough time for this important work can be awfully frustrating (especially if you don't have good notes). Save yourself the hassle by scheduling time to write reviews well in advance. I also like scheduling at least one additional work session to polish my reviews. My first drafts can be unclear or tactless. A second round solves that.

- **What's the most important feedback you want to get across?** Before you start writing, decide for yourself: What do I most want to convey? What do I want the person to get out of my feedback and take away from our talk? Try to get this clear in your mind before writing it out. And leave out any vague or less important feedback, or anything that could be misinterpreted.

- **No surprises.** A good rule of thumb when writing reviews is that none of your feedback should come as a surprise. It should all be familiar from your weekly one-on-ones. Assuming that's the case and you have a good rapport with your team member, you won't be covering any new ground in the feedback meeting. Instead, you can focus together on opportunities for growth in the months ahead.

- **Take time to read other people's feedback.** At Blendle, we set deadlines for each round of reviews to give everyone time to prepare properly. Sounds obvious, I know. But when people have gone to the effort to write feedback, it's extra important to take time to read it through and let it sink in. So make time in your calendar. Before the meeting, try to clarify for yourself the main points you want to convey.

A sincere, thoughtful, and honestly written review combined with an open and positive dialogue can have a huge impact on a team member's performance, the team as a whole, and you.

Finding good people

As a manager, you're usually juggling a lot at once. But no matter how deftly you coach your team, there comes a point when your team is giving all it's got and you realize you need another pair of hands. Turns out, finding that pair of hands is an art in itself.

In 2017, I'd spent a lot of time expanding the team. Afterward, I felt we were caught up and I let my recruiting efforts slide. But at some point in 2018, we spotted areas that could use some new people. Because I'd put talking to new people on the back burner, I had to start the whole process from scratch. That slowed things down considerably and we had to just plug away, understaffed, for a few tough months. Don't make my mistake. Make it a point to always be on the lookout for exceptional people. That means you're talking to new people and nurturing your network. If you wait until you need someone, you're really too late.

The higher up the ladder you are, the more of your time should go into people and hiring. That's because hiring is what's known as a multiplier: you can take all sorts of small steps to work smart and more efficiently yourself, but find the right people to help you out and your effectiveness will take off. And working with good people is the greatest gift you can give yourself as a manager. It makes your work infinitely more interesting.

For managers and non-managers alike, it's good to realize your current network could be a rich source of potential future colleagues. So go ahead and invite people for coffee, forge new connections, and invest in relationships. Besides being fun, a good network is a great resource to have at your disposal.

So, how do you go about finding the right people? Here are some things that can help:

- **Write a clear and honest job description.** Although lots of potential candidates aren't job-hunting and you'll need to cast a wider net (more on that in a moment), it's still important to post a full and inviting job opening online. You can then point interested candidates to that ad. At Blendle, we got the idea of including a summary of concrete challenges the new hire would get to work on. This made a refreshing addition to the same old lists of skills and duties, and applicants were enthusiastic. We also used Homerun, a fantastic online tool that results in professional-looking job posts, makes it easy for people to apply, and keeps track of who's in which phase of the application process.

- **Be prepared to do your own sourcing.** By sourcing I mean pro-actively searching for promising candidates yourself. Why? Because the best candidates aren't job-hunting—they're content where they are. It's up to you to find them, get them excited about your team and organization, and persuade them to get better acquainted. For tips, see the box on the next page.
- **Prioritize diversity.** You can fill a book about this bullet alone. The bottom line? A diverse team is a better team. Beware of hiring more people just like you. Work to bring together a mix of people with different backgrounds, genders, and personality types.
- **The first candidate is almost never the winner.** Here's something that's happened to me a lot. I'm busy recruiting for a new job and the first candidate feels like an instant bull's-eye. It's tempting to stop and declare the winner then and there. But that's rarely a good idea. Instead, I've found I need to talk to at least two or three candidates to compare. As I do more interviews, my perception of the job and that first candidate always changes.
- **Always talk to references.** Talking to one or two of a candidate's references is an easy way to do an extra check. It gives you some

more insight into how that person works. And while there are no guarantees, references might just give you that piece of information you need to make your final choice. For the candidate, it's a sign you're taking their application seriously.

- **Never choose alone.** When selecting new additions to the team, it's always a good idea to enlist other people. Ask someone from a different department to sit in on interviews to see which candidate is a good fit with the larger company culture. If there's no one in the organization who can give that kind of input, tap someone in your network instead. Some of my friends will happily interview candidates over the phone to give me that extra input. (Only if the candidate agrees to the call, of course.)

- **When in doubt: don't hire.** If not everyone at the interview is excited about a candidate, that's a sign to call it quits. No matter how desperately you need someone on the job, a candidate who doesn't meet the team's standards will only create more work.

Sourcing

Some tips for finding candidates:

- **Use LinkedIn, Twitter, and other social networks.** When looking for software developers at Blendle, we always kept an eye on GitHub—an online community for developers—and posted monthly links to our job openings on *Hacker News*, a busy developer news site. Then there's Meetup.com, for meetups that cater to all kinds of interests, from aficionados of a particular sport to app developers, giving us a valuable pool of potential candidates. Whatever the job, there's always a site where good candidates congregate. So check out who's active, read their posts and profiles, and you'll soon have a list of prospects.

- **Use a system to keep track of candidates.** There are plenty of options out there, from Google Spreadsheets to different software packages. hellotalent.com lets you save profiles for potential hires. Trello's another good one. Since applications tend to multiply fast, you need a good system that keeps any from slipping through the cracks.

- **Write original messages to potential candidates.** Ever got one of those messages from a recruiter that spelled your name wrong and made zero effort to be personal? Here's what I do instead: I have a file with some standard paragraphs from which I choose an opening sentence and company intro. But then I tailor the text to the person I'm writing. There's always a way to make it personal. You could bring up one of their past employers, or mention your shared enthusiasm for snowboarding (which you saw on Instagram), or tell them you liked one of their blog posts. That shows you're not just hitting send but took the time to compose a thoughtful message.

In short: make time to find good people. Do that, and your team will soar.

YOUR PROCESSES

As a manager, you're responsible for supplying quality products or services. And for supplying them fast. To do that, you need a solid team and a solid process. From Donald Reinertsen's slightly dry but excellent book, *The Principles of Product Development Flow,*

I learned that there are two dials you can turn to fine-tune your workflow: *lead time* and *cycle time*. *Lead time* just means how long a task is on hold before you can start on it, and *cycle time* is how long it takes until the task is done.

Now to reach your own management goals and supply your products or services, two factors are important to know. First: How long does the work take? And second: When or where is the work getting stuck? What's the holdup? If you have a good team, then understanding the work process may be enough to improve the working method. But if that doesn't do the trick, then detecting sticking points in your team's process is a good start. What can you suggest that would boost efficiency? Are there certain steps that take extra time (like approval from someone outside the team)?

There are so many things that can make work take longer than it should, but in many cases I've noticed the culprit isn't the work itself. Very often, communication *about* work is where you can shave off the most time. That dovetails well with a principle I learned from the podcast *Manager Tools*: your work isn't done until you're done communicating about it. That's become my motto for any team I work with.

These last few years have shown me how crucial it is to keep the fine-tuning process going. And one tool helps make sure I do: my *weekly startup*.

Your weekly startup

Team meetings are the clear choice for getting everyone moving in the same direction. But they soon add up and become a drain on your team's time. That's why I try to be sparing with meetings.

That said, weekly startups are a nonnegotiable for me. They're vital for my team, to get us all on the same page. As the name implies, I do weekly startups first thing Monday morning. Ninety minutes will do it.

I like to start the agenda in a shared Google Document. That way everyone can access the most up-to-date version and suggest new items. We also use a Google Presentation for our weekly startup. Rather than starting from scratch each week, we reuse the same presentation and just update the slide details. More on those in a moment.

My weekly startup has six elements.

1. CHECK IN

I like to open startups with a quick round where we each share how we're feeling and how our weekends went. This isn't just small talk, but an important glimpse into how the team's doing. Before adding this to our weekly agenda, there were times we didn't realize until late in the meeting that someone's irritability stemmed from a rough weekend or unresolved frustrations from the previous week. That often affected the flow of the discussion and decision-making, and not in a good way. Now that we "check in" with each other first, our meetings go much more smoothly. Of course, you also don't want meetings to turn into therapy sessions. You can guard against that by limiting your check-in to about ten minutes at the start.

2. DATA

In the next part of our weekly startup, my team and I run through our *key performance indicators*, or KPIs, from last week.

This data is collected by our data analyst and added to our Google Presentation before each meeting. Ideally, these data points tie in directly with your goals (from those questions you answered at the beginning of this bonus chapter).

3. AN OUTSIDE PERSPECTIVE

Besides reviewing the quantitative data, my team and I always need to be in the loop about what users think of our product. To help us do that, we read the support team briefing each week, which outlines user questions and comments. Having that direct line on what's happening around us is important to me. The support team sums up last week's highlights in a couple of slides that we add to our presentation. As we go through the highlights, we decide what response is needed. Say, if someone found a problem in our app that needs fixing. This part of our weekly startup is great for sharing information from all kinds of stakeholders. And by making room for this information at the startup, the group's clear on what has priority.

4. ONGOING PROJECTS

For this fourth item we take a look at all the projects we're currently working on. At Blendle that includes tests we're setting up and things like expansions of Blendle Audio. Each project gets one slide in the Google Presentation stating the name of the project, the owner (team member), deadline, status, what the project's about in one line, and planned next steps. We talk through each slide so everyone's up to date and can pitch ideas and ask questions.

Project: Adyen ➡ Stripe

Owner: Nora

Deadline: upsell & onboarding – Feb. 21

Status: on track

What: switching Android payments from Adyen to Stripe

- Currently in rollout

5. TO BE DISCUSSED

After running through our projects, we move on to the rest of the items on our shared Google Docs agenda.

6. CLOSING ROUND

The final part of our weekly startup is to quickly go around the team one by one and answer these questions:

- What's your top priority this week?
- Focus and priorities: Do you think the team's working on the right things?
- Problems: Anything you're concerned about?
- Motivation: What are you excited about this week?

One of the best additions to our weekly startups, this brief set of questions offers an easy way for people to raise any doubts or questions they have. And closing with what's motivating us this week ends the meeting on an upbeat note.

Of course, not everything in our weekly startup will be relevant for yours. Start small and add elements you think might enhance your own team meetings. The idea is to embrace experimenting and make changes as you go.

Hello, micromanager

A weekly startup is an excellent tool for directing your team's workweek, but of course a manager's job doesn't stop there. You also have to keep an eye on how the work's progressing. But how much direction should you give? How much input is too much? When is it time to delegate? Full disclosure: I'm a details guy. Deciding when to be hands-on and when to step back is an ongoing struggle. That can get interesting, because delegating the right jobs to the right people is an essential part of my job as a manager. There's a well-known theory on this phenomenon developed by Paul Hersey and Ken Blanchard called the *situational leadership* model. In the simplest terms, the model says this: Has a person mastered the task? Then step aside and let go of the work. Is a person still learning the ropes? Then offer more guidance and direction.

I certainly haven't perfected the art of delegation and management, but it's become increasingly clear to me that the essence of good leadership is to truly *see* your people, and to adjust your style and methods to the folks you're working with. Which is exactly what Hersey and Blanchard say.

Here are some more takeaways from their model:

- **Don't confuse motivation with expertise.** For me, this was the biggest insight about *situational leadership*—that enthusiasm and energy don't always equal knowing *how* to do the job. If you're not sure whether a team member knows how to do something, don't be afraid to ask how they intend to tackle it.

- **Get into the habit of asking more questions.** This is where I like to start. Asking questions gives you a quick way to find out whether someone's clear on what needs to happen, so you know if they need a hand. At the same time, it's a chance to discover that person's unique ideas and make way for them.
- **Agree on delivery deadlines.** As managers, we often hesitate to fix deadlines for what needs to be delivered when out of fear of infringing on our team's freedom. But I advise separating the two. Where the work's concerned, your team members are the experts, but without deadlines all your team's other urgent business is more likely to get done first. What also helps me is planning check-ins to review progress together, say midway through a project. And most importantly, if other people are counting on your team to deliver on a deadline you've agreed to with them, then share that deadline with your team—the sooner, the better. Why? Because if you don't, you're guaranteed to stress yourself out. You'll be getting worked up about your team's progress while they seem to be taking their sweet time.
- **Tell your team *why* you have a hard time letting go.** If you're obsessed with details like me, it's worth asking why. For me, it gets worse when my team's not updating me as much as I'd like and when I'm in a bigger rush than they realize. Both are easily remedied.

It may not come naturally, but there's a happy medium between micromanaging and letting the chips fall where they may.

And if you ask me, that's the essence of being a good manager: knowing how much direction to give each individual and when to get out of the way. Of course, just because you're not spelling out exactly what needs to happen doesn't mean you can't stay involved and know what's going on. But, generally speaking, once the expected outcome is clear, be as hands-off as possible. If you want more granular ideas on this topic, I recommend Hersey's timeless book *Situational Leadership*.

YOUR PRODUCTS

This chapter wouldn't be complete without also zooming in on your products or services: the *what* that you supply. Clearly you'd be nowhere without your team and a solid work process, but if people aren't buying what you have to offer, all that hard work's for nothing. As a manager, you have a tremendous influence on how well your products or services succeed. Often more than you might think. Here's the trio of tactics I use:

Tactic 1: Create focus in your team

The single most important lesson I've learned as a manager to achieve quicker wins is: *do fewer things at once*. My method is all about choosing where to invest your time, but as a manager you also play a key role in your team's focus. Here are two paths to more focus:

- **Be your team's gatekeeper.** You can help your team get more done by keeping distractions at bay. The more hours your team can spend on what's most important, the more effectively they'll work. Makes sense, right? Try proactively heading off things that aren't relevant—like saying no to requests that have no bearing on your team's goals, or nixing pointless meetings they're expected to attend.

- **Be your team's compass.** You make decisions about what your team works on, but your team members are also constantly making choices about what to tackle next. Are they making the best choices? Ongoing input from you helps your people discern what's important. Weekly startups are the perfect time to share those priorities, as are one-on-ones, but it needn't stop there. Get creative about how and when you communicate your priorities.

Tactic 2: Make time to think

It's tempting for managers to do whatever's in front of us at the moment. After all, those emails, tasks, and problems aren't going to take care of themselves. In many cases you're the only one who can address them. And the first thing that tends to get sacrificed in the process is your time to think. That's not only a shame, it can be disastrous in the long run. Granted, you need to get that other work done, too, but the trick is to set aside time for what matters most. Want to supply better services and products? Then set aside some time to think about the bigger questions involved. Is that easy? Absolutely not. But it's just the kind of thing that can give you an edge and boost your team's progress. These three practical tips help me make time to think:

- **Make a list of big issues.** Keep a list somewhere (in your to-do list or notes app) of the big things you want to think about. Anytime one of these issues crops up in conversation, park it on your list.

- **Set aside ninety-minute blocks for thinking.** It's easier if you actually set aside time in your calendar for the specific issues you want to think about. I used to block a whole morning or afternoon for "thinking," but that didn't give me the structure or incentive to make good use of the time. So I switched to ninety-minute blocks, which give me just the right sense of urgency to get my brain in gear. And after an hour and a half, my brain needs a break!
- **Find another spot to do your thinking.** In this book I've talked about all the contextual factors that can influence the quality of your work, like the time of day and the layout of your workspace. When it comes to time to think, see what happens if you find a different spot to work. And you can reinforce that effect by making it routine. So, if you choose to do all your brainwork at the kitchen table at home or at a favorite café instead of the office, that setting alone will put you in the right frame of mind.

Tactic 3: Seek out advice

For most of us, this tactic falls into the category of "I know I should do this, but I don't." It involves getting advice and analyzing alternatives. I cover this approach in chapter 9 (about smart listening) and chapter 10 (on solving problems). In brief:

- **New project? Get yourself some fresh advice.** Whenever you want to start on a new challenge, it's a good idea to talk to at least one person outside your organization. That could be a mentor you know well, or an expert you're consulting for the first time. Either way, this relatively small time investment at the start can save you from getting into all kinds of trouble. And it can take your work to new heights.

- **Surround yourself with sources of information.** There are times a manager's job feels more like that of an air traffic controller. Your pilots are making the spot decisions, but you're the one keeping the whole show in the air. To do that, you need access to all kinds of inside and outside information. In other words, you need a dashboard that brings all the info together. Not only internal data (How's the project coming along?) but also external (What's the competition doing? Who are the front-runners in my field?). Make sure all of this information comes your way. Subscribe to key newsletters and keep up with relevant websites.

Throughout this book, I've shown that you create clarity and peace of mind when you start with a good system, and then adapt it as you go. I'm convinced that goes for managing teams too. You get the most out of a group when you run meetings that work (and scrap those that waste your people's time). Your team performs at its best when you invest in your relationship with each individual team member and find ways to keep shared goals front and center for everyone. Leadership is far from easy, but I hope my pointers help you find new ways to make things run a little smoother. So you can keep from getting bogged down in the day-to-day, and instead set your sights on where you're all headed together.

RECOMMENDED READING

It's tempting to offer a long list of reading tips, just because there's so much great stuff out there. Instead, I'm going to limit my recommendations to three short books. Each can be read in an hour or two. All three are on my list of books to scan yearly, and they never fail to inspire.

STEVEN PRESSFIELD—*DO THE WORK*

If you get stuck in a project, this book will help. Pressfield coaches you past your insecurities, doubts, and misgivings, and his book guides you to get the job done.

ARNOLD BENNETT— *HOW TO LIVE ON 24 HOURS A DAY*

This book, written over a hundred years ago (and which I also cite in the first chapter), is a powerful call to look critically at how you spend your time.

JAMES ALLEN—*AS A MAN THINKETH*

This book reveals how your thoughts influence how you feel and what you get done. It's an inspiring guide to developing your thinking.

Want to dig deeper into a specific theme? I've posted an extensive list of recommended reading on my website: gripbook.com/books.

SOURCES

CHAPTER 1

I learned a lot about time management and using a calendar from the podcast *Manager Tools*: https://manager-tools.com.

•••

Stephen Covey writes about the Eisenhower Matrix and juggling priorities in *The 7 Habits of Highly Effective People*. His insights were invaluable for this book.

•••

The book *How to Live on 24 Hours a Day* by Arnold Bennett inspired the section, "Treat your calendar like a fitness regimen."

CHAPTER 2

Getting Things Done by David Allen was a huge source of inspiration for my second chapter on working with a smart to-do list and the principle of not storing things in your head.

•••

Thinking, Fast and Slow by Daniel Kahneman taught me the distinction between instinctive or rote thinking, which he refers to as *system 1* thinking, and the more conscious, rational thought he calls *system 2* thinking.

•••

In his book *Deep Work*, Cal Newport writes extensively about concentration strategies. His book inspired my *hyperfocus* motivator.

CHAPTER 3

I borrowed the strategy of reading emails three times a day from the *Manager Tools* podcast: https://manager-tools.com.

•••

I learned a lot about addiction from *The Power of Habit* by Charles Duhigg and *Hooked* by Nir Eyal.

● ● ●

The book *Irresistible* by Adam Alter inspired me to dig deeper into the research on email use and to make email a key element of my working method.

CHAPTER 4

The Friday recap in my method is based on David Allen's "weekly review" in *Getting Things Done*.

CHAPTER 5

The *skills* puzzle piece is based on the "craftsman mindset" in *So Good They Can't Ignore You* by Cal Newport.

● ● ●

Start with Why by Simon Sinek taught me a lot about why *why*'s a good place to start.

● ● ●

Organizational Behavior (2012), published by the Saylor Academy (saylor.org), offers a great overview of motivation theories on which I based my *passion*, *skills*, and *mission* puzzle pieces: https://gripbook.com/link/motivation.

● ● ●

From *Drive* by Daniel Pink I learned about the value of having a mission.

● ● ●

The term "Big Hairy Audacious Goals" is taken from *Switch* by Chip and Dan Heath.

CHAPTER 6

Chris Guillebeau's blog on *How to Conduct Your Own Annual Review* inspired me to start doing my own Year Plan Days: https://gripbook.com/link/annual-review.

CHAPTER 7

Jeff Sanders's blog on *Best Topics for a Weekly Accountability Partner Meeting* made me see the tremendous value of finding a partner in crime: https://gripbook.com/link/accountability.

CHAPTER 8

The book *Peak Performance* by Brad Stulberg and Steve Magness taught me about energy, stress, and overloading.

CHAPTER 9

I learned the basics of smart listening from Stephen Covey,

who writes about this in "Understand Before Being Understood," in his book *The 7 Habits of Highly Effective People.*

● ● ●

I also learned a lot about listening from the *Manager Tools* podcast: https://manager-tools.com.

CHAPTER 10

The "Five Whys" method was originally developed by Toyota to get to the root of production problems.

● ● ●

The four-category classification of bias comes from Buster Banson and his article, "Cognitive Bias Cheat Sheet:" https://gripbook.com/link/bias.

CHAPTER 11

The book *Clock of the Long Now* by Stewart Brand gave me a fresh take on time and inspired the final chapter.

THANKS

Everything in this book is some combination of lessons learned, books read, and ideas tossed around with good friends and the people I was lucky enough to work with. In bringing the best of all that together, I hope it helps take you further than you've ever been. You wouldn't be holding this book in your hands if Alexander Klöpping and Ernst-Jan Pfauth hadn't pushed me to publish it. I'm forever grateful to Harminke Medendorp for helping me straighten out my thoughts into a coherent and accessible story, and to Ruth Bergmans and Maarten Richel for helping me make it a big success in Holland. Erica Moore and Elizabeth Manton took the book to a whole new level with this fantastic English translation. Whenever you think *that's a nice line*, it was them. I want to thank the monks from St. Willibrord's Abbey in the Dutch town of Doetinchem for providing a quiet place to think and write—I hope to return there for many years to come. And thank you to Derk, who's been my partner in crime since 2014. His weekly pep talks pulled this project over the finish line. I've spent enough words on the concept of accountability sessions before, but the finished book is a testament to a practice that works. I hope our weekly talks never end. Finally, I'd like to thank my beautiful wife, Joàn, for giving me the space to explore my crazy projects.

NOTES

Chapter 1

1. Paul Graham, "Maker's Schedule, Manager's Schedule," 2009. http://www.paulgraham.com/makersschedule.html.

Chapter 2

1. Gloria Mark, Victor M. Gonzalez, and Justin Harris, "No Task Left Behind? Examining the Nature of Fragmented Work," Take a Number, Stand in Line, Portland, Oregon, April 2005. https://www.ics.uci.edu/~gmark/CHI2005.pdf.

2. Taylor Trudan, "How Rumaan Alam Used a Secret Twitter Account to Write the Book of the Year," Shondaland, October 7, 2020. https://www.shondaland.com/inspire/books/a34277128/rumaan-alam-leave-the-world-behind-interview/.

3. Michael Chui, James Manyika, Jacques Bughin, Richard Dobbs, Charles Roxburgh, Hugo Sarrazin, Geoffrey Sands, and Magdalena Westergren, "The Social Economy: Unlocking Value and Productivity Through Social Technologies," McKinsey Global Institute, July 1, 2012.

Chapter 3

1. A fascinating study by IBM Research tracked 345 users that collectively conducted over 85,000 "refinding actions." The study concludes that sorting email in folders (or tags, for that

matter) is both ineffective and inefficient. Using a search function, in combination with email software that supports threads, both saves time and increases successful refinds. Steve Whittaker, Tara Matthews, Julian A. Cerruti, and Hernan Badenes, "Am I Wasting My Time Organizing Email?" Proceedings of the International Conference on Human Factors in Computing Systems, CHI 2011, Vancouver, BC, Canada, May 7–12, 2011. https://www.researchgate .net/publication/22151 8713_Am_I_wasting_my _time_organizing_email.

Chapter 5

1. Check out this article where setting goals leads to a clear improvement in the work that was done. That study builds upon many other studies that have a similar conclusion: setting goals helps you focus. Marieke van der Hoek, Sandra Groeneveld, and Ben Kuipers, "Goal Setting in Teams: Goal Clarity and Team Performance in the Public Sector," *Review of Public Personnel Administration* 38, no. 4 (2018). https://journals .sagepub.com/doi /full/10.1177/0734371 X16682815#_i15. Not convinced by studies that focus on business targets? This recent study found that goal setting in sports affects effort, persistence, and direction of attention. Kingston Kieran and Kylie M. Wilson, "The Application of Goal Setting in Sport," *Advances in Applied Sport Psychology: A Review*, no. 1 (2009), 75–123. https:// journals.humankinetics .com/view/journals/jsep /7/3/article-p205.xml.

2. "'You've Got to Find What You Love,' Jobs Says," Stanford University, June 14, 2005. https://news.stanford .edu/2005/06/14/jobs -061505/.

3. The original report from 1981 by Locke, Latham, and others says: "A review of both laboratory and field studies on the effect of setting goals when learning or performing a task found

specific, challenging goals led to higher performance than easy goals, 'do your best' goals, or no goals." Edwin A. Locke, Karyll N. Shaw, Lise M. Saari, and Gary P. Latham, "Goal Setting and Task Performance: 1969–1980," *Psychological Bulletin* 90, no. 1, 125–152. https://psycnet .apa.org/record/1981 -27276-001. Locke and Latham haven't stopped doing research. In a fascinating 2019 article, they explain their process and new insights in detail. It's a great starting point for exploring other studies on setting goals. Edwin A. Locke and Gary P. Latham, "The Development of Goal Setting Theory: A Half Century Retrospective," *Motivation Science,* 5, no. 2 (2019), 93–105. https:// doi.org/10.1037/mot 0000127.

4. Gail Matthews, "Goals Research Summary," 2015. https://www.dominican .edu/sites/default/files /2020-02/gailmatthews -harvard-goals-research summary.pdf.

Chapter 6

1. Chris Guillebeau, "How to Conduct Your Own Annual Review," chrisguillebeau .com, 2008. https:// chrisguillebeau.com/how -to-conduct-your-own -annual-review/.

Chapter 7

1. Humphrey Carpenter, *J. R. R. Tolkien, A Biography* (Unwin Paperbacks, 1978), 152.

Chapter 10

1. You can read them at https://gripbook.com/link /onboarding.

2. Buster Benson, "Cognitive Bias Cheat Sheet," busterbenson.com, 2016. https://busterbenson.com /piles/cognitive-biases/.

Chapter 11

1. Rick Pastoor, "The Risky Business of Onboarding," *A List Apart,* July 14, 2015. https://alistapart.com /article/risky-business -of-onboarding/.

2. Rick Pastoor, "Get People on Board," Webdagene, 2016. https://vimeo.com/188134881.

3. Stewart Brand, *The Clock of the Long Now: Time and Responsibility* (Basic Books, 1999).

Bonus Chapters

1. My thanks to Lucas Reinds, Eric de Vos, Thomas Smolders, and Arjan Broere for sharing their tips.

2. gripbook.com/link/blendle-feedback.

ABOUT THE AUTHOR

Rick Pastoor has always liked experimenting at work. He'll try things out, then keep what works, ditch what doesn't. Try. Rinse. Repeat. In his time at Blendle, the *New York Times*–backed journalism startup, Rick steadily refined his methods. That's where GRIP was born, a flexible collection of tools and insights that helped the team do their best work.

Originally self-published in Dutch in 2019, GRIP became an overnight bestseller in Holland. Rick's mission today is the same: helping people make smarter decisions about their time. He divides his own time between his young family in Amsterdam, giving talks on GRIP, his weekly newsletter *Work in Progress*, and a new startup, where he's building a next-generation calendar called Rise.

Find more from Rick at rickpastoor.com and gripbook.com.